# LIFE DURING COLLEGE

## Valuable Advice & Tips For Success

**John Ricchini, MBA, CPA**
**Terry Arndt, MBA**

Life After Graduation, LLC
5645 Kathryn Street • Alexandria, Virginia 22303
(877) 569-9816 (Toll-Free)
info@LifeDuringCollege.com
www.LifeDuringCollege.com

# DEDICATION

This book is dedicated to our extremely understanding, patient and beautiful wives, Jennifer Ricchini and Melissa Arndt. Thanks for allowing us the opportunity to chase a dream. We would also like to say "thank you" to everyone who supports our company and is making our dream come true.

## ABOUT THE AUTHORS

John Ricchini and Terry Arndt met while attending the University of Florida MBA program where they had both received a concentration in Entrepreneurship. While brainstorming ideas for their class business plan, John and Terry focused on the one quality in which they had the strongest bond - a desire to be frugal. This quality proved successful for John and Terry. Not only did they receive a great grade for their business plan, but they also developed a successful company with two great products. The company, Life After Graduation, LLC, produces "Life After Graduation" and "Life During College."

**John J. Ricchini** is currently employed as a Manager of Financial Planning and Analysis at the University of South Florida Physicians Group. Prior to his current employment, John was a healthcare consultant at a "big five" accounting firm, a financial manager at a physician management corporation, as well as auditor with another "big five" accounting firm. John earned his MBA degree from the University of Florida and a Bachelor of Science degree in Accounting and Finance from LaSalle University. He is a Certified Public Accountant in the State of Pennsylvania and is currently pursuing a Charted Financial Consultant designation from The American College.

**Terry J. Arndt** is currently employed as an Assistant Director of Membership and Marketing for an industry trade group in Washington, D.C. Prior to his current employment, Terry worked as a sales representative for several years in the agriculture industry. During his career in sales, Terry attended a number of training courses in sales and negotiation techniques offered from world-renowned companies. Terry earned his MBA degree from the University of Florida and a Bachelor of Science degree from Washington State University.

## USING "LIFE DURING COLLEGE"

"Life During College" is the perfect product to be given as a gift, to raise money for a worthy cause, or to use as reference material for a freshman orientation program. To find out how you can use "Life During College," visit us on the Internet at www.LifeDuringCollege.com or call us toll-free at (877) 569-9816 for more information.

## OTHER BOOKS BY THE AUTHORS

Life After Graduation: Financial Advice & Money Saving Tips

## COPYRIGHT INFORMATION

## BOOK DISCLAIMER

The authors of this book and Life After Graduation, LLC have made their best efforts in preparing this book to be accurate and complete. The content of the book is not guaranteed to produce any particular results. In addition, the advice given in the book may not suit every individual's circumstances.

Therefore, the authors and Life After Graduation, LLC do not assume responsibility for advice given. As a result, each reader should consider their own circumstances and abilities and weigh them versus the advice given.

The authors and Life After Graduation, LLC are not in the business of rendering financial, legal, or any other professional advice. If any questions regarding legal or financial advice should arise, the reader should seek professional assistance.

The authors and Life After Graduation, LLC shall not be held liable for any damages arising from the book's content.

# CONTENTS AT A GLANCE

# TABLE OF CONTENTS

# TABLE OF CONTENTS

# TABLE OF CONTENTS

# TABLE OF CONTENTS

# TABLE OF CONTENTS

# HOUSING TIPS
# YOU CAN LIVE BY

## CHAPTERS

# LIVING AT HOME

Living at home while going to college has its advantages and disadvantages. One of the primary advantages of living at home is the financial savings. By living at home you can save a considerable amount of money primarily from housing and food costs. However, the biggest disadvantages of living at home during college are the lack of freedom, inability to learn how to live on your own, as well as the risk of not having a true connection with your college. If you do choose to live at home while attending college be sure to consider the following.

**Develop A Plan With Your Parents**
Living at home while going to college can create situations that neither you nor your parents have faced previously. The following tips will help you and your parents address these situations before they occur and make living together during your time at college a positive one.

- Address financial concerns, such as paying for food and utilities.
- Discuss your class, study and extracurricular activities with your parents so that they understand your schedule. In addition, ask your parents about their scheduled activities and address conflicts that may occur.
- Consider your use of the telephone, Internet and computer while attending college. These are essential tools for a college student and it may be best to have your own telephone line, Internet service and computer available to minimize conflicts.
- Ask your parents about what they expect from you while living at home, such as tasks they want you to perform or rules they want you to follow.

# ON & OFF CAMPUS HOUSING

In some cases, where you live during your first year at college may already be determined for you, since many colleges require their freshman students to live on campus. However, where you live for the remainder of your time at college is often up to you to determine. This section will provide you some of the advantages and disadvantages of living on and off campus. In addition, this section will provide you information on a few important issues you will need to address regardless if you live on or off campus.

## 1. PRIMARY ADVANTAGES & DISADVANTAGES
### On Campus Housing
*Advantages*
- Housing is usually centrally located on campus, providing easy access to classes, libraries, study areas, and other campus resources.
- Commuting is limited, if needed at all. If needed, commuting can usually be accomplished with public transportation.
- Meals are typically provided through the college catering service.
- The college typically provides cleaning services for common areas, such as hallways, bathrooms and study rooms.
- The college usually provides resident assistants/advisors for each of the college's on campus housing locations to help residents with problems they may encounter, such as a roommate problem.
- All of your services (heat, air-conditioning, water, trash and sewer) are usually included in your housing fee. The only additional fees you may be required to pay are for telephone and cable service, if these services are allowed.

*Disadvantages*
- Roommates may be chosen for you, particularly during your first term.
- Privacy is limited since many areas of the building are shared, such as the bathrooms and entertainment rooms.
- Meal services are usually only offered during certain times of the day. For example, breakfast may only be available from 6:00 a.m. through 9:30 a.m.
- Meal selection may be limited. For example, if you were craving meatloaf for dinner, the college catering service may not be offering it on the day you want it. In addition, receiving special food services may be difficult, such as a diversified vegetarian or diabetic menu.
- You may need to leave your building in order to find a quiet location to study.
- Rules regarding the activities that take place in your room and building are determined by the college and must be followed or you risk being evicted.
- Some on campus housing may not be equipped with cable or telephone service. If not, these services may be offered in a central location within the building for all residents to use.
- Visitors and pets may not be allowed, and if they are, the rules tend to be very restrictive.
- If you have a car, you may have to pay for a parking permit in order to park your car on campus.

## Off Campus Housing
*Advantages*
- In many cases, living off campus is less expensive since you are not being provided all of the extra services that the college offers to on campus residents.
- Choosing the location of where you want to live and who your roommates will be is your choice.
- You and your roommates establish the rules regarding the activities that can, and can not, take place in your living area.
- The living area of off campus housing tends to be much larger than on campus housing.
- Private bathroom, bedroom, kitchen, and common area
- Pets may be allowed.
- Personal parking space(s) may be included.

- A clothes washer and dryer may be included in your personal living area, thus avoiding the need/use of a laundromat.
- You choose what you want to eat and when you want to eat.
- Personal telephone and television service capability.

*Disadvantages*
- The responsibility for starting and stopping services, such as water, sewer, trash, garbage, telephone and cable, is yours.
- Purchasing groceries, preparing meals, and cleaning your living area are your responsibility.
- You will need to commute to campus, which increases your time and expenses.
- Limited access to campus resources and interaction with other students
- When problems arise, such as a problem with a roommate or neighbor, there may not be someone available to help you resolve the problem.

## 2. GREEK LIVING
A popular form of on campus housing is living within the Greek system. Although somewhat similar to other forms of on campus housing, the Greek system has its own distinguishable advantages and disadvantages. To learn more about these, and other aspects of the Greek system, read the "Greek Life" section on page 92.

## 3. ROOMMATES
Whether you decide to live in an on or off campus housing environment, roommates are often a fact of life, and getting along with your roommate is important. Having a poor relationship with your roommate will only add stress and tension to your life. To avoid this, be sure to follow some of the recommendations in this section.

### Contact Your Roommate Prior To Moving In
Whether you know your roommate or not, you should contact him/her before you move in. Take this opportunity to introduce/re-introduce yourself. Once you feel comfortable with your roommate, start discussing housing issues, such as establishing new services (cable, telephone, etc.) or decorating ideas. In addition, you may want to establish rules in order to avoid conflicts. Try not to dominate the conversation and appear overwhelming by inviting your roommate to offer suggestions.

Finally, if you are easily upset by certain actions/situations, bring them up with your roommate so that those particular conflicts can be avoided.

## Avoid Judging A Person On Your First Impression

In some situations, particularly if you will be living on campus, you may not know who your roommate is. Visiting with your new roommate on the telephone or meeting them in person for the first time can be shocking. The best way to handle visiting or meeting someone for the first time is to avoid making assumptions. In most cases, assumptions are wrong. Therefore, be open-minded and allow the relationship to develop.

## Roommate Does Not Always Equal Friendship

In most situations, particularly if your roommate is chosen for you, your roommate will not become your best friend. However, this does not mean that you cannot be friends. Living with a new person is an opportunity to learn and experience new thoughts and ideas, to see how someone else views life. Take advantage of this opportunity and if you gain a new friend in the process, even better.

## Living With A Friend Or Relative

Deciding to live with a friend or relative may seem like a great option; however, it may not always be the best option. For example, although you may think that you know everything about your best friend from high school, do you know if he keeps his home as clean as yours? Never assume that just because you are friends, or that your roommate is a relative, that your relationship will fix disagreements. Treat your living arrangement with your friend or relative like you would with any other roommate. Doing so will help your relationships grow even stronger.

## Establishing Rules

Establish rules between you and your roommate as soon as possible. Rules provide structure and organization to your living environment and assist in avoiding and resolving conflicts. When establishing rules, make the process a group effort. Avoid dominating the conversation by inviting your roommate to make suggestions or offer comments. Also, never downplay or make fun of rules that are suggested or comments that are made, and always respect the rules that are agreed upon. You may find it helpful to review the rules occasionally to add new rules or adjust old rules. Rules you should consider discussing include:

- Quiet time for studying and sleeping
- Use of the telephone line for Internet and/or telephone calls
- Cleaning duties and responsibilities
- Overnight guest policies
- Privacy and property rights

## Communicate With Your Roommate
Communicating with your roommate is the only way disputes and disagreements can be resolved effectively. Communication is best when it is done face-to-face. Doing so will help avoid confusion and will also allow each person involved the ability to address his or her concerns. Although communications with your roommate can also be accomplished with a written note or email, these are less effective than communicating face-to-face.

If you are living on campus, your Resident Advisor/Assistant will usually assist you if you are having difficulty communicating with your roommate. However, if you are living off campus, it is often up to you and your roommate to develop an open line of communication.

## Respecting Your Roommate's Privacy And Property
In order to develop a strong relationship with your roommate you must respect each other's privacy and property. Be sure to discuss privacy and property issues with your roommate early on in your relationship and determine what you both expect from each other. If you are concerned about any issues related to your privacy or property, you should inform your roommate about them immediately. Doing so will help avoid embarrassing situations and/or potential conflicts.

## Changing Roommates
In some situations, differences between you and your roommates may never be resolved. If this situation occurs, consider these recommendations.
*On Campus Housing*
- Review the college's policies regarding changing roommates. Your college housing department can assist you in locating this information and informing you of your responsibilities.
- Contact your Resident Advisor/Assistant about the situation and request assistance.

*Off Campus Housing*

Changing roommates in an off-campus housing situation is a bit more difficult than on campus housing scenarios. The reason is that there is often a legal contract (lease) involved. Therefore, resolving conflicts correctly is important so that legal and financial errors can be avoided. Listed on the next page are some options to consider when dealing with an off campus roommate conflict.

- Review your lease for any issues relevant to your situation. If necessary, you may want to contact your landlord for assistance.
- Contact a college counselor or your college's student legal center (if available) for assistance.
- One option available, if both you and your roommate's names are on the lease, is to determine if the lease agreement can be assigned to a new person. If so, you or your roommate may be able to get out of the lease if someone else is willing to take over your financial and legal responsibilities.
- If all else fails, you and your roommate may need to decide to break the lease, split any fees associated with doing so, and each of you go your separate ways.

## 4. TRANSPORTATION

Transportation is an important component of determining where you will live while attending college. Although how you get to and from campus depends a lot on personal preference, there are a number of other factors to consider. Listed below are just a few of them.

### Methods of Transportation Available

When evaluating locations to live, particularly for people without personal vehicles, having access to different methods of transportation is important. For example, does public transportation, such as a bus route or subway system, service the area and/or is the area conducive to bikers and walkers.

### Parking

For most campuses, finding a parking space is a luxury and if you can find a space, you usually have to pay a lot for it. Therefore, if you are considering living off campus and plan to drive to school, be aware of the school's parking system. For example, is parking difficult to find during the hours you are planning to be on campus? If parking permits are required, what is the cost? Are there parking spaces available near your classes?

**Commuting**
One major advantage to on campus housing is that your commute to classes is minimal. Therefore, when deciding to move off campus, be sure to keep the amount of time you are willing to spend commuting to and from campus in mind.

**Transportation Expenses**
One expense that is often not included in the comparison of on and off campus housing options is the transportation expense. Often, by living on campus your transportation expenses are very minimal. However, this can be quite different for students living off campus. If your budget is tight, as it can be for most college students, be sure to include transportation expenses into your calculations when comparing your options for places to live. If you own a personal vehicle, be sure to include average maintenance and insurance expenses, as well as gas in your calculations. Also, be sure to consider car-pooling as an option to help reduce your expenses.

## 5. FOOD
For some students, food can be the deciding factor when choosing between on and off campus housing. Planning your meals, purchasing your groceries and preparing your own meals can be a bit overwhelming when comparing it to a program, such as a college meal plan, where you simply pick what you want to eat and pay for it. However, this convenience does come at a price. Therefore, as you compare your options for places to live, be sure to consider these tips.

- Investigate the meal plan options that your college offers and locate the plan that best meets your needs.
- Be aware of your ability to adjust your meal plan during a term and/or your ability to carry credit on your meal plan from one term to another.
- Some colleges allow students who do not live on campus to purchase meal plans. If so, and you are interested in using this service, be sure to consider your schedule and the times that the food service will be available before choosing a meal plan.
- When comparing a college meal plan to purchasing your own food, you may find it helpful to write out an average meal plan for yourself for a one-week period, and then go to the local grocery store and calculate what it would cost you to purchase that food yourself versus purchasing it on the college meal plan.

- Be aware that part of making your own meals is preparing and serving your meals. Therefore, food preparation and serving materials, such as pots, pans, plates, and utensils, will need to be purchased if you do not already own these materials.

## 6. LEGAL & FINANCIAL RESPONSIBILITIES

Whether you decide to live on or off campus, you will need to accept a number of legal and financial responsibilities. Listed below is advice and tips regarding your legal and financial responsibilities.

### Legal Responsibilities

The two primary legal responsibilities that most college students need to be aware of when finding a place to live are signing a lease and protecting their valuables. For many college students, signing a lease is usually their first major legal responsibility. Both on and off campus housing providers will require you to sign some form of a lease. To learn more about leases and their legal ramifications, review the "Renting An Apartment" section on page 11. As for protecting your valuables, in most cases, your parents' homeowners insurance will cover any losses. However, you should have your parents contact their insurance provider to ensure that your valuables are included in their coverage. If not, ask your parents, family members, or friends for assistance in locating a reputable insurance provider that can help you with your insurance questions. In some cases, your college may offer special insurance programs for students. Contact your college's Student Services office for more information.

### Financial Responsibilities

Living on your own is a big financial responsibility. Although most on campus housing programs offer a simple one-payment plan, where all your services are included in one payment, you may still be responsible for other services, such as telephone and cable service. As for off campus housing, your financial responsibilities will also include telephone and cable service, but may also include items such as utilities (gas, electric, water and sewer), garbage service, and security deposits. When deciding where to live, be aware of the estimated expenses associated with places that you are considering living. Most off campus housing complexes can provide you this information. However, contacting each of the service suppliers directly for this information may provide you a better estimate of the expenses and deposits that you can expect to pay.

# RENTING AN APARTMENT

Renting an apartment can be expensive, frustrating and time consuming if not approached properly. Not only do you need to be concerned with finding an appropriate apartment, but you also need to be aware of the rental process. Therefore, whether you are searching for an apartment to rent, or you are already renting an apartment, you should review the suggestions and techniques described in this section to save yourself time and money.

## 1. PRIOR TO RENTING AN APARTMENT

Before you begin looking for an apartment, there are several important questions you need to answer.

### What Is Your Budget?

Understanding your budget constraints is essential to determining what apartments you can even consider renting. By reviewing the "Budgeting" section on page 115, you should have a clear picture of your financial resources. Be sure to include miscellaneous expenses related to your apartment as you complete your budget, such as furnishings, telephone and cable service, and Internet access.

### Where Do You Want To Live?

In most cases, your apartment budget often will dictate where you can live. For example, in general the closer you live to campus, the more expensive the apartment will be. Before you begin to look for an apartment, get a map of the area and begin outlining optimum locations to live, such as close to campus or near some form of public transportation. To assist in minimizing your apartment search, contact apartment complexes and visit with friends that are located in the areas you are interested in living to determine the average rental price.

## 2. LOCATING AN APARTMENT

Once you have determined your budget and the locations that you prefer to live, you can start looking for an apartment. There are several resources to use when searching for an apartment.

• **Newspaper Classifieds**
Both the local and school newspapers will usually have a classifieds section dedicated to apartment rentals. Some even have expanded listings to break-up the options to include furnished and un-furnished apartments.

• **Internet**
There are a number of Internet Web sites to assist you in locating apartments in an effective and efficient manner. These Web sites allow you to search for an apartment based on numerous criteria, such as location, number of bedrooms and bathrooms, pet restrictions, and price range. To locate these Web sites, simply use any of the various Internet search engines and enter the words "apartments" or "rent" in the search field.

These Web sites may offer toll-free telephone numbers in order for you to contact the apartment directly. If you do not have the time to contact each apartment directly by telephone, several Web sites allow you to request information on-line.

• **Bulletin Boards Around Campus**
A lot of apartments are still advertised the old-fashioned way – with a bulletin board. Although you should be skeptical of these postings, great deals can be found using this method.

• **Apartment Locator Companies**
Owners of apartments will often use the services of companies that specialize in finding qualified tenants for their apartments. These companies pre-qualify potential tenants and are often involved in the signing of the rental agreement. The owner of the apartment will provide the locator company a "finders fee/commission" for each apartment they fill; therefore, the apartment locator service is often free of charge for the potential tenant.

- **Realtors**

In many communities, realtors provide rental listings as well as "for sale" properties.   As with apartment locator companies, realtors make their compensation for showing rental properties from the "finders fee/commission" provided by the rental owners.   Contact realtors in your area to determine if they provide rental listings.

- **Friends/Classmates**

One of the best ways to find a great apartment is by word-of-mouth from friends and classmates.   Let your friends and classmates know that you are looking for a place to live and ask them if they know of any great places. Someone is bound to know of a place that will meet your needs.

- **Apartment Guide Publications**

In larger communities, you can often find a listing of available properties in apartment guide publications.   These publications are usually located near newspaper stands or outside retail markets.    One benefit of these publications is that they provide you with a detailed description of the properties and their amenities.   However, these publications are usually produced in large quantities and are not updated regularly.

## 3. SELECTING AN APARTMENT

After you have located a number of apartments that you want to look at, prepare a checklist of your needs and preferences.  A sample checklist is provided on the next page.   Fill in the checklist as you visit different apartments.  Doing so will help you recall the positive and negative aspects of each location easily and allow you to better evaluate all of your choices at the end of the day.

| Descriptions & Amenities | Apt. 1 | Apt. 2 | Apt. 3 | Apt. 4 |
|---|---|---|---|---|
| Neighborhood (Rate 1-10) | | | | |
| Cleanliness (Rate 1-10) | | | | |
| Dishwasher (Yes/No) | | | | |
| Washer/Dryer (Yes/No) | | | | |
| Parking Space (Yes/No) | | | | |
| Property Location (Ground, Top Floor, End Unit, etc.) | | | | |
| Length Of Rental Agreement | | | | |
| Monthly Rent ($ Amount) | | | | |
| Separate Bills For Each Roommate (Yes/No) | | | | |
| Proximity To Campus (Rate 1-10) | | | | |

## 4. NEGOTIATING WITH LANDLORDS

The amount of negotiating power you have is directly correlated with the number of rental properties available. If there are a lot of properties available for rent, the better negotiating power you have. However, this does not mean that if there are a limited number of rental properties available you have no negotiating power. It simply means you must be more creative when negotiating. Below are a few suggestions to assist in negotiating the rates of rental properties:

- If you believe that you will live in a particular area for an extended period of time, consider signing an extended lease. This may reduce your monthly rent or provide you with a significant discount on your first month's rent.
- When negotiating the terms of your lease, be sure to mention competitive rental rates from the area, specifically any promotional advertisements that a competitor is offering. Be sure to mention this even though you may prefer the apartment complex that you are visiting. Let them know that you are an informed shopper and want to be given competitive terms.

- When negotiating the security deposit, if a full-month's rent or more is required as a security deposit, negotiate to have that amount reduced. If you are not able to receive a discount on your security deposit, request to have the amount of the security deposit paid in installments made over two or more months. Suggest this option even if you have sufficient funds available. This will enable you to have more flexibility with your funds when establishing your new home.
- When negotiating for a reduction in monthly rent or the security deposit, be sure to provide a reason for your request, such as the incredible financial strain you will incur by moving and establishing a new home during that initial month. Your reasoning may prompt the landlord to offer you the deal.
- Other negotiations can be made without discussing discounts. For example, you can condition your offer to rent the property on the replacement of new carpet or linoleum, or some other change. (Be sure to have any agreement put in writing.)
- If you are signing a time-oriented lease (i.e. twelve-month lease), request to continue your lease on a month-by-month basis after the lease expires.

## 5. FREE-RENT PROMOTIONS

The competitive nature of the rental property market plays a significant role in the type of promotional deals a rental property offers. In a competitive environment, it is common to have rental properties offer the first month's rent for free or for a significant discount. These promotions generally occur in larger cities and college communities with abundant housing.

The free month's rent or reduced rent promotions may occur only during certain times of the year. Therefore, be aware of when these offers occur, as signing a lease at the right time may save you a significant amount of money. If you live a good distance from the rental property location, ask the landlord if they are currently offering such promotions. You can also contact the area Chamber of Commerce to ask when, and if, such promotions are available in that community.

## 6. REPAIRS/SERVICES FOR REDUCED RENT

Renting an apartment from a private individual has its advantages. Unlike most large apartment complexes that are owned by management companies and have an existing staff of maintenance employees, local landlords depend on local businesses to supply the repair services for their properties. This situation can result in a unique opportunity for the renter.

Due to the expense, time, and coordination of hiring local businesses to provide repair services, landlords are interested in alternatives to avoid this hassle. Therefore, if you have a fair amount of experience performing small repairs, such as painting or yard work, inform your landlord of your skills. You might be able to negotiate a discount in the rent during months in which you perform repair work. Do not sell yourself short for providing these services; however, do not become too greedy. Also do not agree to provide services you are not competent in performing, such as rewiring electrical outlets or repairing heating elements in a stove. You do not want to create the need for additional costly repairs.

## 7. SIGNING THE LEASE - A LEGAL PERSPECTIVE

In most cases, a rental agreement is the first legal contract many college students enter into. The most important thing to remember before signing a lease is that, if there is a disagreement or conflict, all resolutions will be based on the legal document (contract) that you and the landlord signed. Therefore, if the lease does not reflect oral agreements that you made with the rental property management, it is your loss. Below are some important steps to undertake prior to signing a lease.

- Read the lease thoroughly. In fact, it is recommended to take the lease and review it in private before signing it.
- When reviewing the lease, highlight areas on the lease that you are unsure about, or have questions regarding the meaning, and be sure to have them addressed.
- If the lease contradicts what was said to you during your meeting with the landlord, have them specify which version is correct – the lease or what was said. Be sure the lease reflects the correct version.
- If agreements are made regarding repairs to be made to the property or on what basis the security deposit will be refunded, be sure that the lease reflects those agreements prior to signing. For example, if the landlord states that new carpets will be put into the rental property prior to occupancy, be sure to write that into the lease and have the landlord sign or initial that version before you sign.

- If you agree to a month-by-month lease once the initial terms of the lease are completed, have that specified in the lease.
- If you have a roommate(s), determine whose name(s) is going to be on the lease. Remember that, if your name is the only name on the lease, you are ultimately responsible for the lease payments. By not making your monthly payments you could potentially hurt your credit rating (see the "Credit Report" section of page 129). Therefore, consider having all of your roommates sign the lease. Furthermore, if you have not established a credit history, you might need your parent(s) to co-sign the lease. Therefore, consider having a few parents co-sign the lease to distribute the responsibility to each roommate(s)' parents.

## 8. MOVING INTO YOUR APARTMENT

You should follow these suggestions before moving into your new apartment:

- Always walk-through and review your apartment closely for all the items that are not operating properly or are defective prior to moving in. For instance, notify the landlord of stains in the carpet. Create a detailed list of all imperfections. Some rental properties have their own form for you to list damages on. If this form does not provide sufficient space for listing the damages, continue the list on a separate sheet of paper. Be as detailed as possible. Also be sure to note on the original form that a separate sheet containing further damages has been attached. Once you complete this task, sign the documents and obtain the signature of the landlord. Have two copies of the signed documents made - one for property management and one for you.
- If the apartment has not been cleaned or does not meet the specifications provided for in your lease, inform the landlord. Request that the needed services be completed immediately. Also request a discount or credit on your rent for the delay in your move and/or for the inconvenience you suffered.

## 9. MOVING OUT OF YOUR APARTMENT

The following are a few tips to follow when you are moving out of your apartment:

- Even if management does not require a "walk-through" of your apartment before you move out, request to have your rental property manager/owner walk through your apartment prior to your moving out, so that you are aware of any potential charges against your damage deposit.

- Once the walk-through is complete, request that the rental property manager/owner sign your damage report (that you filled out when you moved in) and state what, if any, charges will be deducted from your security deposit.
- Many apartment complexes will charge a standard non-refundable fee to have your apartment cleaned upon your departure. In almost all cases, this fee is stated in the lease and is usually reasonable and will guarantee that you will not be charged for any cleanliness problems.

## 10. SUBLEASING

Before agreeing to sublease your apartment, consider the risks you are subjecting yourself to. The laws in many states provide that the signer of the lease is liable for any damages that occur throughout the term of the lease while you are a resident, or after you turn the rental property over to another tenant under the sublease. Therefore, if the person to whom you sublease the rental property creates a significant amount of damage, (beyond what the damage deposit covers), and fails to pay for those damages, the landlord has the legal right to hold you liable for those damages. Therefore, instead of subleasing your rental property, consider finding someone that will sign a new lease. This will relieve you of all legal aspects of your lease. However, the landlord must agree to terminate your initial lease.

If the rental property manager/owner does not approve of starting a new lease with a new tenant in order to release you from your current lease, consider accepting the expense of terminating your lease early. Most leases specify penalties for terminating the lease. In many cases, terminating a lease early is far less expensive than paying for damages caused by a subleaser.

# MAXIMIZING YOUR EDUCATION

## CHAPTERS

# ACADEMIC ADVISORS

Colleges provide students with academic advisors to assist them in getting the most out of their college experience. This chapter will help you understand who academic advisors are, what they do, as well as what your responsibilities and options are when being advised.

## 1. WHO ARE ACADEMIC ADVISORS?

Academic advisors can be one of the following types of individuals:
- Full-time faculty within your designated major
- Professional advisors solely dedicated to advising
- A combination of full-time faculty and professional advisors

## 2. ACADEMIC ADVISOR RESPONSIBILITIES

Academic advisors provide assistance with the following:
- Scheduling/changing/dropping classes and elective courses
- Selecting/changing majors and minors
- Organizing classes to meet graduation requirements
- Providing information about campus activities
- Assisting you as needed to meet your career goals

In addition to these responsibilities, academic advisors can also provide you with updates on course changes, new graduation requirements, as well as alternative courses that you can take. Also remember that academic advisors will keep all of your information confidential.

## 3. STUDENT RESPONSIBILITIES

Although academic advisors are available to provide assistance with your college experience, they are only there to assist you. Remember, you are ultimately responsible for the choices that you make regarding your college experience. The following items will help you get the most out of meetings with your advisor, as well as make the most of your college experience.

- Be aware of the time periods that your academic advisor makes available for advising and try to schedule your meeting well in advance in case you decide to make additional changes to your schedule at a later date.
- Be on time for your meeting with your academic advisor as it may be difficult to reschedule. In addition, you do not want your advisor to get the impression that you do not believe their time is important to you.
- Bring a list of questions for your academic advisor so that all of your concerns and questions are addressed.
- Bring a planner or appointment calendar to schedule additional meetings if necessary.
- Bring a copy of your most recent transcript to your meeting so that your advisor has a clear understanding of your academic progress.
- Ask your advisor for their opinion on courses that you are interested in taking and be open to suggestions. Also, remember to be respectful of your advisor's opinions and suggestions.
- If possible, get your advisor's answers/recommendations in writing so as to minimize misunderstandings later on.

## 4. LIMITATIONS OF ACADEMIC ADVISORS

Although academic advisors do have a wealth of information to offer in assisting you with your college experience, they may not have all of the answers. It is not uncommon for advisors to be unfamiliar with new courses or with course options outside their area of expertise. Therefore, you may need to schedule meetings with professors or other advisors to obtain a better understanding of courses that you are interested in taking.

## 5. CHANGING AN ACADEMIC ADVISOR

On occasion, you may find that your current academic advisor does not meet your needs, particularly if you change majors. If you are in a situation where you believe you need to change your advisor, consider some the following items.

- Before deciding to change your academic advisor, visit with your favorite professor(s) about your situation and ask for their recommendation. In addition, schedule meetings with different academic advisors to discuss your situation and determine if they can better meet your specific needs.
- After locating an academic advisor that will better meet your needs, be sure to visit with them about how to go about officially making them your designated academic advisor.
- If your request for an academic advisor change is denied, schedule a meeting with the dean of your college to discuss the situation and present your reasons for requesting the change.

# CHEATING –
# IT IS NOT WORTH THE RISK!

Every college has specific policies regarding cheating, as well as the consequences students will face if they are caught participating in this activity. These policies are usually provided in your student handbook. In addition to the policies enforced by the college, many professors have the ability to implement their own policies related to cheating. **Simply put, do not cheat!** To avoid putting yourself in a position where cheating may occur, this section will describe the reasons cheating occurs, provide examples of several different forms of cheating, and discuss the consequences that you can face if you cheat.

## 1. WHY DO STUDENTS CHEAT?
There can be a number of reasons a student may decide to cheat. For example, they may be under tremendous pressure from their parents to do well in school or they may feel overwhelmed by the demands of a course they need to complete successfully in order to graduate. Whatever the reason, there is always a better alternative to cheating.

For example, if for some reason you are under extreme pressure to do well in a course and you are having difficulty with the materials, try visiting with your professor about the situation. In many cases, the professor will personally work with you to assist you in completing the course successfully. However, if you are unable, or uncomfortable, in visiting with your professor about your situation, visit with your academic advisor or a school counselor and ask for their assistance.

## 2. FORMS OF CHEATING

Review your college's policies on cheating to be sure you are aware what is, and what is not cheating. If you are ever unsure, ask your professor or academic advisor. Below are a few samples of the more common forms of cheating.

- Plagiarizing a book, article, or Internet Web site
- Turning in an assignment completed by someone else for your own credit
- Copying from someone or allowing someone to copy from you
- Arranging to have someone take an exam on your behalf or taking an exam for someone else
- Giving or receiving signals for answers during an exam
- Asking students who have already completed the exam before you about the content of the exam
- Storing any information into an electronic device, such as a scientific calculator or watch, that may assist you with the exam

## 3. CONSEQUENCES OF CHEATING

Unlike students in high school who cheated and may have been sent to detention as their punishment, college students are subject to much more severe forms of punishment, including being expelled. To learn about your college's punishment for cheating, refer to your student handbook.

In some cases, the professor alone may reprimand a student who is caught cheating. However, many colleges require that their professors report any form of cheating to the college's administration. Students who are accused of cheating are usually provided the opportunity to defend themselves to the department head, college administration, or even a student court. If the student is found guilty of cheating, they can face a variety of punishments, including failing the course they were caught cheating in, being put on suspension, or even being expelled. A copy of the proceedings, if the student is found guilty of cheating, is also added to the student's school records, which can cause considerable difficulty for the student to be accepted into another college or to pursue an advanced degree.

Finally, never assume that if you cheated during college, and you receive your degree, that you are safe. There have been many instances where graduates have had their degrees revoked after the college determined that the graduates had earned their degree by cheating.

# COLLEGE RESOURCES

Your college offers you a number of resources to make your college experience as educational and fun as possible. In order to take advantage of these resources, you need to understand what resources are available, as well as how those resources can assist you. Provided below are some of the more common college resources that are available to students, as well as a description of how these resources can assist you. Although most colleges have these resources available to their students, some colleges may combine services or refer to them with different titles. To find out what resources your college provides, refer to your student manual or contact your academic advisor or counselor for assistance.

## Academic Advisor
Colleges provide students' access to an academic advisor in order for the student to get the most out of their college experience. The advisor's primary goal is to map-out the student's long-range goals and then develop an academic calendar in order for the student to have the education they need to achieve their goals. Please refer to the "Academic Advisors" section on page 20 for more information about the services and responsibilities of your Academic Advisor.

## Admissions Office
The Admissions Office is available to assist prospective students in obtaining and completing the information that is needed to fulfill the admission process for the college.

**Alumni Association**
The Alumni Association's goal is to make sure that the alumni of the college have access to the college through a variety of channels. This is accomplished by developing various services and programs that are only available to college alumni, such as special discounts, free email accounts, or other services. Alumni Associations are also a great resource to use when networking. See the "Networking" section on page 141 for more information.

**Bursar**
The Bursar is the primary service unit for managing the financial records and needs of the college, including its students. This is the location where students often pay their bills.

**Career Services**
The Career Services Office provides students the resources they need to decide upon and plan for a career, as well as conduct job searches. To provide these services, the Career Services Office may conduct seminars, job fairs, as well as informational events on resume development, job interview skills, and networking.

**Counseling Center**
The Counseling Center is a service provided to students who are in need of assistance or who do not know where to go or who to talk to about problems/situations they are involved with – either school-related or otherwise.

**Financial Aid Office**
The Financial Aid Office is available to assist prospective and current students in financing their educational expenses.

**Greek Affairs**
The office of Greek Affairs supports the educational and social learning goals of the fraternities and sororities that are located on the college's campus. Functions can include advising and encouraging academic success, diverse membership recruitment, leadership development, community service, risk management, and sound maintenance of physical facilities.

## Multicultural Affairs

The office of Multicultural Affairs provides support services for multicultural students to assist them in achieving their educational goals. In addition, the office of Multicultural Affairs works to create an environment on campus that acknowledges, respects and enhances multiculturalism.

## Ombudsman

The role of the ombudsman is to provide a neutral and informal resolution to problems that arise in the college setting. For example, if your professor assigned you grades that you believed to be unfair, the ombudsman would look into the situation, at your request, and provide a resolution to it.

## Registrar

The Registrar is primarily in charge of course scheduling, but also manages the issues related to scheduling, such as fee waivers, residency and enrollment issues, transcripts, grade reporting, and billing.

## Residence Life

The primary role of the Residence Life Department is to maintain housing and dining facilities and programming in support of the on-campus community. This includes developing meal plans, planning room assignments, and matching roommates.

## Student Activities Center

The Student Activities Center's role is to provide students with information about activities and events that are available for students on and off campus, such as intramural sports, white-water rafting trips, and more.

## Student Government

The primary purpose of the Student Government is to represent the concerns and interests of its students, as well as to provide programs for the improvement and enrichment of the campus community.

## Student Health Care Center (Health Center)

Student Health Centers provide quality, affordable and accessible health care to students.

# GOALS

Goals play an important part in your life. They are used as tools to make yourself, and the environment in which you live, better. Therefore, developing, accomplishing and evaluating goals should become an important component of your college career. This section will assist you with the process of developing, accomplishing, and evaluating goals to make your college experience successful.

## 1. WHAT IS A GOAL?

A goal is an aim or objective that you wish to accomplish. Listed below are a few examples of some types and lengths of goals that you may want to develop during college.

### Types Of Goals

The most common types of goals college students develop for themselves are academic, personal and social goals. Below are a few examples of each.

- Academic Goals
  1. Earning a specific Grade Point Average (GPA), such as a 3.6 GPA
  2. Attending every class and being on time
  3. Preparing for every class by completing reading and homework assignments on time and reviewing notes from the previous class
- Personal Goals
  1. Maintaining a regular diet and exercise program
  2. Maintaining a financial budget
  3. Staying in touch with your friends and relatives on a regular basis

- Social Goals
  1. Obtaining a leadership position in a club
  2. Being an integral member of your intramural football team
  3. Volunteering time to your favorite charity

**Lengths Of Goals**

The length of time it takes you to accomplish your goal is up to you. The most common terms referred to for accomplishing goals are short- and long-term.

- Short-Term Goals
  Short-term goals usually encompass smaller tasks that must be accomplished in order to reach a larger, long-term goal. They can be over a period of days, weeks or months.
- Long-Term Goals
  Long-term goals are goals that are reached through a process of accomplishing a number of short-term goals or processes over a period of weeks, months or years.

*Example:*

A student determines that she wants to obtain a 3.5 cumulative GPA during her freshman year of college as her long-term goal. In order for her to accomplish her long-term goal, she must complete a number of short-term goals that she has developed for herself. These include developing a weekly study group for each of her courses, spending at least 2 hours studying for each class that she attends, and scheduling one-on-one meetings with all of her professors at least every three weeks to discuss her progress and understanding of the materials in the course.

## 2. BENEFITS OF DEVELOPING & ACCOMPLISHING GOALS

The primary purpose, or benefit, of developing goals is to provide direction and structure to your life. Without this direction and structure, you may become overwhelmed or lose focus on what you need to do in order to accomplish a particular task. In addition to the direction and structure that developing goals provides, the process of accomplishing goals provides greater self-confidence, a sense of pride and achievement, and reduces stress and anxiety.

## 3. DEVELOPING & ACCOMPLISHING YOUR GOALS

Simply writing your goals down on a sheet of paper and hoping that you achieve them is not enough. In order to successfully accomplish a goal, you must develop a plan outlining the steps you must undertake in order to accomplish it. The following tips will assist you in developing and accomplish the goals that you have established for yourself.

- **Prioritize Your Activities**
  Extra time is a luxury that most college students do not have. Therefore, review your daily, weekly and term (semester/quarter) schedule to determine how best to utilize your time. You may find it helpful to review the "Time Management" section on page 82 for more information on developing your schedule and prioritizing your activities.

- **Avoid Negative Goals**
  Negative goals, or goals that you dread working for, are goals that you are most likely not going to accomplish anyway, such as doing 300 sit-ups per day. Instead, set goals that you want to accomplish and are willing to dedicate your time and effort to. Goals that you want to accomplish are goals that you will accomplish.

- **Be Specific**
  When developing your goals, be as specific as possible. For example, instead of stating that you will spend more time studying for your Macroeconomics course, state that you will spend two hours studying for every hour of Macroeconomics lecture.

- **Develop Measurable Goals**
  If possible, develop goals that provide tangible evidence of your efforts. For example, instead of establishing a goal to do well in your Chemistry course, establish a goal that you will obtain a grade of a "B" or better in your Chemistry course. By doing so, not only will you be better able to determine what actions you need to undertake in order to achieve your goal, but you will also be better able to judge your success.

- **Challenge Yourself**
  Avoid establishing goals that you know you can achieve with little effort. Instead, challenge yourself. Remember, the purpose of establishing goals is to motivate yourself to do better, not to maintain a status quo.

- **Be Realistic**
  Although the purpose of establishing goals is to motivate yourself to do better, you should not establish goals that are impossible to achieve. Evaluate your skills and abilities and develop goals that you believe you

can accomplish. For example, if you worked hard, but struggled with understanding the materials in your Chemistry 101 course and thus, received a grade of a "C," establishing a goal to receive a grade of an "A" in your Chemistry 201 course is probably not realistic.

- **Establish A Time Frame**
  Without a set time frame for accomplishing a goal, the more likely that goal will not be accomplished. By establishing a time frame, you are developing an environment that will remind you to complete the tasks needed in order to accomplish your goal.

- **Create Reminders**
  Remind yourself of the goals that you have established. Writing your goals on a sheet of paper that you hang on your wall or noting them on your calendar are great reminders. By constantly reminding yourself of the goals that you have established, the more likely you will stay focused and the less likely you will fail.

- **Positive Reinforcement**
  Create an environment that provides a positive reinforcement. This will assist you in keeping on track to accomplishing your goals. For example, if your goal is to obtain a grade of an "A" in your Chemistry 101 course, take assignments and exams that you did well on and place them where you can see them frequently, such as on the wall where you study.

## 4. EVALUATING YOUR GOALS

Evaluating your goals allows you to monitor the progress towards obtaining your goals, providing you the opportunity to make necessary adjustments so that you can successfully complete your current and future goals.

The key to evaluating your goals is to remember that your goals are not etched in stone and that they can be adjusted. Thus, if a situation occurs that causes you to be unable to accomplish your goal unless you implement changes, then make the changes. Although adjusting your goals is not an ideal situation, remember that even though you had to make an adjustment, you still accomplished your goal. For example, say you established a goal to study for at least four hours each weeknight. After the first three weeks of this program your part-time job employer makes you adjust your work schedule so that you are unable to accomplish your study goal on Tuesday and Thursday nights. Instead of dropping your goal altogether, simply adjust your goal to rearrange the hours that you will study, such as sticking to the original goal of four hours a night on Monday, Wednesday, and Friday, two hours a night on Tuesday and Thursday, and four hours on Saturday morning.

The process of evaluating your goals is not just for goals that you are currently completing. You should also evaluate the goals that you have already accomplished. When evaluating goals that you have accomplished, look for areas that you had difficulty accomplishing or for schedules that you had difficulty following. Also note if you needed to adjust your goals in order to accomplish them, or if the goals that you had set for yourself were too difficult or too easy to accomplish. As you consider these points, be sure to keep them in mind as you establish new goals for yourself so that frequent adjustments to future goals will not be needed.

# GRADES

Grades are an important component of your college career. So much so, that they can determine how your future will evolve. Scholarship committees, college department advisors, graduate school entrance administrators, as well as employers, all use grades as a guide to help them determine if a student is qualified to receive the benefits that they have to offer. This section will provide you with information on the importance of maintaining good grades, as well as the options that may be available to you if you receive a poor grade.

## 1. DEVELOP A GOOD FOUNDATION

Developing a good foundation with good grades in your prerequisite courses will allow you to be better able to handle struggles that may occur later in your more difficult courses. In addition, many scholarship committees, college department advisors, graduate school entrance administrators, as well as employers, judge you on your progress, not your end results. Therefore, starting with a good foundation is vital to your success.

Consider the example of Student A and Student B on the next page. Both students take the exact same courses, but begin their college careers with two different foundations. Student A works hard and receives a strong 4.0 Grade Point Average (GPA) in her prerequisite courses, establishing a strong foundation. On the other hand, Student B enjoys too many extracurricular activities during her first year at college and puts little effort into her prerequisite courses. This provides Student B with a weak 2.0 GPA foundation. Although in the end, Student B does finish her college career with the exact same GPA as Student A, Student B must work much harder in the more difficult courses in order to accomplish the same GPA as Student A.

| GPA | Student A | Student B |
|---|---|---|
| Freshman Year | 4.0 | 2.0 |
| Sophomore Year | 3.5 | 3.5 |
| Junior Year | 3.0 | 4.0 |
| Senior Year | 3.0 | 4.0 |
| Final GPA | 3.4 | 3.4 |

Although this is a fairly simple example, it does show that taking advantage of earlier prerequisite classes to establish a strong foundation will make your life much easier as you proceed through the harder courses later in your college career.

## 2. GRADES ARE NOT EVERYTHING
Although having a high GPA is important, it is not the only factor used to judge your accomplishments during your college career.  For example, although scholarship committees, college department advisors, graduate school entrance administrators, and employers do look for candidates that have high GPA's, they also want candidates who possess other talents, such as leadership and communication skills.  Participating in a variety of extracurricular activities can help develop those skills.  However, participating in too many extracurricular activities can be detrimental to your grades.  Therefore, create a mix that you are capable of accomplishing successfully.  You may want to refer to the "Time Management" section on page 82 and the "Career Preparation" section on page 133 for more information.

## 3. IMPROVING YOUR GRADES
Poor grades can be caused by any number of factors.  This book provides valuable information to assist you in determining what may be the cause of your poor grades and what steps you should take to improve them.  Review the following sections to assist you in improving your grades.

- To assist you in determining the cause of your poor grades, consider visiting with your professor or academic advisor. See the "Professors" section on page 47 and "Academic Advisors" section on page 20.
- To learn how to study more effectively, review the "Studying" section on page 62, as well as the "Note Taking" section on page 39 and "Textbooks" section on page 78.
- To determine if you are using your time effectively for studying, review the "Time Management" section on page 82.
- To improve your test taking skills, review the "Taking Exams" section on page 68.

## 4. CHALLENGING YOUR GRADES

Occasionally you may encounter a situation where you believe an assignment or exam was graded incorrectly, or a question on the assignment or homework was improperly stated, which in turn caused you to answer it incorrectly. Whatever the situation, if you have a concern about a grade you received, you should challenge it. Below are some suggestions on how to challenge a grade.

- Regardless if you are concerned about a grade or not, it is always a good idea to review all of your assignments and tests for errors in grading.
- If you are concerned about how you were graded on a question, research and develop information to defend your concern. Information that will be helpful in defending your concern includes references to class notes, the course textbook, or previous assignments.
- Schedule an appointment with your professor to review the assignment or exam in question with you. Doing so will not only provide you sufficient time to develop your case, but will also show the professor that you care about the materials and have an interest in doing well in the class.
- If the professor disagrees with your case, avoid becoming defensive or angry. This will not provide you the results you want to accomplish. Instead, have the professor explain their reasoning so that you can understand why you answered the question incorrectly.
- If, after consulting with the professor, you are still not satisfied with the grade, you can usually go one step higher: the department. Usually departments have grade-petition procedures whereby students can appeal to a departmental committee. Consult the departmental office for guidelines.

## 5. THE DROP/ADD OPTION

Most colleges offer students a period of time after the term has begun to drop courses from, and add courses to, their schedules. The drop/add option allows students the ability to experience a class first-hand, and then, if necessary, rearrange their course schedule to meet their specific needs. In addition, the drop option allows students who are performing poorly in a class the ability to drop that class with minor penalties. Before you decide to drop or add a class, consider the following tips.

- Review your college's drop/add policy. While reviewing, be sure to note the time schedule for dropping and adding courses, as well as any penalties that are associated with the process.
- If you are unsure about the college's drop/add policies, contact your academic advisor for clarification.
- If you believe you need to drop a class because of a poor grade, schedule an appointment with your professor to discuss the situation. Your professor may be able to provide you alternatives to dropping the class, such as allowing you to perform extra credit work, providing you personal assistance to help raise your grade, or sending you to a tutor for assistance.

## 6. THE PASS/FAIL OPTION

Some colleges offer students the ability to take a course without a grade designation. Instead of a grade, the student will receive a pass or fail designation. In some cases, students may be able to enroll in a class for a grade designation and then later in the term convert over to the pass/fail designation. For students who are performing poorly in a course, this may be a better alternative than accepting a drop designation on their transcript.

## 7. INCOMPLETE GRADES

Occasionally students are unable to complete a course within the standard term of a course due to unforeseen circumstances, such as a death in the family or health problems. To accommodate students in these situations, most colleges allow students the ability to make arrangements with their professors to complete the course outside of the ordinary term of the course. This process is reflected on the student's official transcript for that term as an "Incomplete" grade. Once the student completes the course and is awarded a grade, that grade will replace the "Incomplete" grade on the student's official transcript.

# LISTENING

Listening is an important and effective skill to develop. In college, effective listening skills will not only assist you in doing well in your courses, but will also assist you while networking and interviewing. This section will first describe the difference between listening and hearing and then it will provide you with some tips on how to become a better listener in class. However, these tips are not just for college. Many of these tips can easily be applied to any situation where effective listening is important.

## 1. HEARING VERSUS LISTENING
Hearing and listening are two very different acts. Hearing is the act of experiencing or being aware of sounds. However, listening is the act of hearing with the intention to understand, to pay attention, or to be influenced by what is being heard.

## 2. TIPS TO BECOME A GOOD LISTENER
A good listener must be motivated and must concentrate on what is being heard. Listed below are some tips on getting motivated and concentrating in order to become a better listener and perform better in your courses.

### Getting Motivated
Getting motivated to listen to a college lecture can be difficult. To motivate yourself to want to listen to, and learn from, a college lecture, develop a reason for why you must do well in the course. In most cases, students must do well in a course in order to receive their degree. If this is the reason why you are taking a course, use this as your motivation for listening. However, if you are taking the course for other reasons, such as to learn a new skill or

to broaden your knowledge base, then use that as your motivation. You may find it helpful to note your motivation on the cover of your course lecture notebook or another location as a reminder.

## Concentrating

Concentrating on a college lecture can be equally as difficult as getting motivated. In some cases, lack of concentration is caused by factors outside of your control, such as a serious illness in the family. However, in most cases, you can control factors affecting your concentration. Listed below are some tips to help maintain your concentration.

- Physical preparation is essential to concentration. Be sure to get enough rest before class, eat healthy meals, and exercise. Read the "Healthy Living" section on page 100 for more information.
- Be prepared for the lecture. Arrive at the lecture room early and bring the tools you need to take notes during the lecture. In addition, be sure to review study materials prior to attending the lecture.
- Avoid distractions during the lecture. Sit near the front of the lecture room where you can see the professor clearly. Also avoid sitting near noisy, or annoying, students.
- Focus on the information being presented. Try to determine potential assignment or exam questions, as well as key points the professor is trying to make. In addition, develop questions to ask about the information being presented.

# NOTE TAKING

Having the proper study tools is essential to an effective study program, since many professors develop a large portion of their exams and assignments from their lectures. Therefore, notes from your classes, labs and study groups may be the most important tools that you can utilize. However, notes are only effective if they provide you with the information you need and are in a format that can be easily used. This section will provide you with a number of tips and methods to use in taking good quality notes.

## 1. PREPARING FOR CLASS

Preparing for class is as important as attending the class. Not only will preparing for class provide you with a better understanding of the materials that are being presented, but you will also be prepared to take effective notes. The following are some tips to help you prepare for class.

### Complete Reading & Homework Assignments

To assist you in understanding the materials that will be discussed in the next class session, your professor will often provide you with various reading and homework assignments to complete. Not only will completing these assignments assist you in understanding and participating in the lecture, but it will also assist you in taking effective notes. In addition, to assist in your note taking, try to remember key terms or phrases and develop abbreviations for them. This will help speed up the note taking process during the next class session by eliminating unnecessary writing.

### Review Your Notes From Previous Class Sessions

Try to spend some time reviewing your notes from previous class sessions. This will assist you in gaining a better understanding of the materials to be discussed as well as provide you with tips on how to take more effective notes for the upcoming class. In addition, by reviewing previous class notes, you can develop questions for the professor to answer during the next class that will help you better understand confusing material.

### Plan To Arrive At Class On Time
Most professors start their class by addressing questions the students may have about materials that were presented in previous class sessions. In addition, they may provide a quick summary/review of the previous class or the current class.

### Bring The Proper Supplies To Class
You can only take effective notes if you have the proper tools with which to take notes. Therefore, spend a few minutes before class to gather the supplies that you will need. In addition, if you use a computer for taking notes, be sure your battery is fully charged in case electrical outlets are not available.

### Sit At The Front Of The Class
Although sitting at the front of the class may seem uncomfortable, it is often the most optimal location. Not only will you be forced to pay attention and take good notes, but when you sit in front, the professor will also begin to recognize you as someone who values the class. This recognition may be important when trying to schedule one-on-one meetings with your professor outside of class, as well as when your professor must decide on your final grade, particularly if class participation is a key component of your grade.

## 2. TAKING NOTES DURING CLASS
Taking good notes during class can be difficult, especially if your professor talks quickly or does not revisit important topics throughout the class. However, by implementing the following tips, you will be able to take effective notes during class.

### Use Abbreviations
As mentioned earlier in this section, try to develop abbreviations for common terms that will be discussed in the class lecture. This can help in speeding up the note taking process and limit unnecessary writing. In addition, utilize abbreviations for more common terms, such as w/ (with), w/o (without), and b/c (because) to limit unnecessary writing. Learning shorthand for the ten or twelve most commonly used phrases from a

shorthand text will save you an immense amount of time in college as well as in your career.

## Write Clearly
Not being able to understand/read your notes is almost the same as not taking notes at all.  If you are having difficulty writing your notes so that you can understand them later, discuss the situation with your professor.

On many occasions, if you are having a problem, there are most likely other students who are experiencing the same situation.  Your professor may offer some advice on taking more effective notes for the class or may even adjust the lecture style to allow students more time to take notes.

## Provide Space For Additional Information
An effective strategy for taking notes, particularly for classes that revisit important topics throughout the class, is to provide sufficient space within your notes for supplementary information, such as questions or additional comments.  In addition, writing your notes with sufficient space often makes your notes easier to read.  Therefore, try to leave space around the margins of your notes as well as between topics.  Also, be sure to bring a sufficient amount of paper to class to avoid running out.

## Listen For Exam Questions Within The Lecture
As professors lecture, they often provide students the exam questions within the lecture itself.  Listed below are clues to listen/watch for in a lecture to help you identify potential exam questions.
- Listen for repetition of points, changes in voice inflections, and enumerations of a series of points.
- Write down any comparisons between items.
- Write down everything that your professor displays on the chalkboard, overhead projector, or in powerpoint.
- Write down information that is repeated by your professor.
- Write down information that your professor gets overly excited about or emphasizes as important.
- Put an asterisk, or other focal point, next to these items to be reminded of the importance of the information.

**Do Not Erase Mistakes**
Mistakes will occur when taking notes. However, try not to waste time by erasing those mistakes. Simply cross the mistake out and continue taking notes.

**Avoid Missing Class**
There are a number of reasons why you should not miss a class, one of which is not being able to take notes. However, situations occur when missing a class is unavoidable. If you must miss a class, you can either obtain notes from a reliable friend or even contact your professor directly and request an outline of the class lecture. Be aware that because everyone has their own style of taking notes and a different opinion of what they view as important, no two students' notes will be the same. Therefore, you should try collecting notes from that day from a couple of different resources and then develop your own notes from them.

## 3. DEVELOPING YOUR NOTES AFTER CLASS
Transforming your class notes into an effective study tool occurs after the lecture is completed. Once the lecture is finished, you should go through the process of reviewing, editing, organizing, and evaluating your class notes. Listed below are tips on how best to perform these tasks.

**Review Your Notes**
Try to review your notes as soon as possible after your class while the information is still fresh in your memory. By doing so, you will be able to expand on topics that you had limited time to develop during class, clean up unclear writing, and look for errors.

**Edit Your Notes**
After class, and before the next class, be sure to edit your notes. The sooner you edit your notes, the less likely you will forget important information. Editing can include expanding your notes by adding information to them from the text book and homework assignments, notes from your study group, or notes from previous exams the professor has provided as study material. In addition, while editing, you can add questions to your notes that you want your professor to expand on during the next class session.

You may find it is most effective to rewrite your notes to include all the information described in the previous paragraph versus just adding it to the notes you took during class. In addition, you may find it helpful to use highlighters or different colors of ink to bring attention to important information.

### Organize Your Notes

After editing your notes, it is important to organize them. An effective method of organizing your notes is to put them in a three-ring binder. Place your notes in sequential order and remember to put the class date the notes are referencing at the top of the page. By placing your notes in a three-ring binder, you can easily insert homework assignments and handouts next to the class notes they refer to. This will not only keep all of your class notes and information in an easy to use format, but will also help you avoid losing important information.

### Evaluate Your Notes

While completing the reviewing, editing and organizing steps, be sure to evaluate your note taking process. For example, while reviewing and editing your notes, did you come across topics you know the professor discussed but you did not include in your class notes? Or, after reviewing, editing and organizing your notes, is there a better note taking format you could use during class? If so, implement the necessary changes and re-evaluate your note taking process again.

## 4. OTHER NOTE TAKING OPTIONS

There are a number of options available for taking notes during class rather than just using a pen/pencil and paper. Listed below are several options to consider.

### Tape Recording

Tape recording lectures can be an effective tool, particularly for classes where the professor speaks quickly or for classes that cover very detailed information. However, if you do choose to use a tape recorder, you should also take notes because putting the information in a format that you understand is much more valuable than listening to hours and hours of tape recordings. Before using a tape recorder, visit with your professor about any concerns they may have with you recording the lecture.

**Video Recording**
Recording a college class on video is becoming more and more popular, particularly for larger colleges. At these schools, classes are recorded and made available for students to view. If your classes are video recorded, utilize them to double check your class notes or review class sessions where information was discussed that you are having difficulty understanding.

**Notebook Computers**
For some people, typing is much faster than writing. Therefore, for these people, using a notebook computer to take notes during class would be much more efficient. In addition, editing notes on a computer is much easier than editing them on paper. If you prefer to use a computer to take notes, visit with your professor before bringing your computer during class.

## 5. REVIEWING YOUR NOTES AFTER AN EXAM
Once you receive an exam back for review, one of the first things you should do after checking your score is to evaluate the questions on the exam. Determine where the materials for the questions were derived, such as from the class lecture, textbook, homework assignments or lab. Then review your notes to find that same material. If you did well on a certain question, evaluate your notes that assisted you in answering that question correctly versus the notes that you had for a question that you did not do well on. If there is a difference in the methods that you used in taking notes for the correct and incorrect question, learn from that difference and utilize those skills when preparing for your next exam.

## 6. PROTECTING YOUR NOTES
As you continue to build-up your class notes and spend hours developing them, the more valuable they become to you, and to others. Therefore, you should take every precaution to protect them from theft, damage or loss.
- Type/save your notes onto a computer.
- Make photocopies of your notes and store them in a safe location.
- Do not allow your original notes to be borrowed - only provide copies.

## 7. SAVING YOUR NOTES
Saving your notes is always a good idea, even after you complete a course. Since many courses build on one another, you may find a need for reviewing your notes at a later date.

# PARTICIPATING IN CLASS

Participating in class, particularly during your first year at college, can seem like a frightening experience. Often, students fail to participate in class because they are concerned about what the other students and the professor will think of them. For example, will other students consider a person who asks questions a "nerd" or "brown-noser"? Or, will the professor think the question is dumb? Although these feelings are normal, they are not justified. For example, many of your classmates are probably experiencing the same feelings as you are. In addition, regardless of the question asked, your professor is usually just happy to know that students are paying attention to the information that is being presented. Remember, you earned the right to be in that class. Knowing this, this section will assist you in understanding the benefits of participating in class, as well as provide you some tips on how to participate in class.

## 1. BENEFITS OF PARTICIPATING IN CLASS

There are numerous benefits to participating in class. Listed below are just a few reasons why you should participate in class.

- Increases your concentration and allows you to stay focused on the information being presented.
- Class participation, for many courses, can make up a significant part of your overall grade. Even if class participation is not technically listed as a percentage of your overall grade in a course, many professors will use your level of participation as a guide in determining your final grade, particularly if your final grade is very close to going to the next higher level.

- Makes the course more enjoyable because you will have a better understanding of the information.
- Increases your self-confidence.

## 2. TIPS FOR PARTICIPATING IN CLASS

As mentioned in the introduction, participating in class can be difficult. However, by following some of these tips, participating should become much easier.

- Prepare for class by reviewing your class notes and completing assignments.
- As you prepare for class, anticipate questions your professor may ask and develop answers for those questions.
- Try to develop several questions to ask for each class. By having several questions available, you will always be able to ask at least one question even if another student asks a question that you had anticipated asking.
- In order to avoid more difficult questions, participate in the discussion that takes place earlier in the class.
- Focus on the quality of your comments and questions versus the quantity. A good method to accomplish this is to keep your comments and questions brief and to the point.
- If you do not agree with a statement made during class, do not be afraid to disagree and/or question the statement. Not only can this add charisma to the class, but it can also assist in your learning process.
- Even if you are not 100% positive about the answer to a question, attempt to answer it. Doing so, even if your answer is incorrect, will help you understand how the correct answer was formulated.
- As soon as you think of a question, write it down so that you do not forget to ask it.
- Refer to your notes or textbook when developing statements or answers to questions.

# PROFESSORS

Developing a positive relationship with your professors is always a good idea. Doing so will not only assist you in your learning process, but it can also provide you with a number of other benefits, both inside and outside of the classroom. This section will describe the different types of professors you may interact with during your college experience, as well as advice and tips on how to develop a stronger relationship with them.

## 1. TYPES OF PROFESSORS
The term "Professor" is often used as a general term when referring to a person who teaches a college course. However, not everyone who teaches a course is a "Professor." In fact, there are several different types of educators that are hired to teach college courses, one of those being a "Professor." Listed below are a few of the more common types of educators that you may encounter during your college experience.

### Professors
College Professors are the highest-ranking college educators. They may, or may not, teach courses (undergraduate and graduate) at the college, and usually conduct research projects for the college. Most College Professors have earned a doctoral degree and have a tenure status (*the right of holding a position that is earned after accomplishing a length of service or by accomplishing a set number of tasks - a person with tenure status can usually only be terminated under specific circumstances*).

**Assistant/Associate Professors**
Assistant and Associate Professors are educators that are in the process of earning their doctoral degree, conducting research, or working toward the requirements to become a full-professor and earn tenure status.

**Lecturers/Adjuncts**
Lecturers/Adjuncts are educators that are usually hired by the college on a temporary basis. They may, or may not, have a doctoral degree and are not eligible for tenure status.

**Teaching Assistants**
Teaching Assistants, also referred to as Graduate Teaching Assistants or Assistant Instructors, are typically graduate students who are currently earning their masters or doctoral degrees. In many cases, they are required to teach as part of their degree requirements. However, Teaching Assistants are usually compensated for their services financially or by having some of their college expenses waived. Teaching Assistants are usually assigned to introductory courses.

## 2. DEVELOPING A POSITIVE RELATIONSHIP
Developing a positive relationship with your professor takes time and effort, but the benefits are usually well worth the investment. Listed below are just a few things you can do to develop a positive relationship with your professor.

- Attend class regularly and be on time. If you are not able to attend class, contact your professor and inform them of the situation. Be sure to ask what materials will be discussed so that you can be properly prepared for the next class session.
- Participate in class discussions. In addition, try to discuss current issues that are related to the course materials during class, such as articles from a newspaper or magazine.
- Ask questions. Professors often use questions from students as a judge of the students interest in the materials as well as a judge of how their particular teaching methods are working.
- Be prepared for class.
- Avoid disruptions and negative attention, such as talking with other students, making or receiving phone calls, surfing the Internet, eating and drinking during the lecture, or leaving class early.

- Turn in your assignments and exams on time.
- Sit in an area of the classroom where the professor will notice you, such as in the front few rows of seats.
- Be sure you address your professor's title and pronounce their name correctly. Professors usually inform students of their preferred title and pronunciation of their name during the first meeting of the course. If you do not know how to address your professor, ask fellow students or contact the departmental office for help.
- Be opened minded and respect the opinions of your professor and other students.
- Do not ask your professor if information that they are presenting will be on the exam. Instead, if necessary, ask what information you should focus more attention on when studying for the exam.
- Get to know your professors by scheduling a meeting with them.

## 3. WHY MEET WITH YOUR PROFESSOR?

There are a number of reasons to meet with your professor on a regular basis. The primary reason is to distinguish yourself from other students in the course. You want your professor to recognize you as someone who is interested in, and enthusiastic about the course materials and who wants to do well in the course. Your time and effort in developing this relationship with your professor will go well beyond just being recognized as someone who is interested and enthusiastic about the course. There are many other benefits that you can gain from this relationship, including:

- Advice on how you can do better on future assignments and exams
- Benefit-of-the-doubt when you have a grade in question
- Access to valuable contacts in the industry that you hope to contact about an internship or job
- Resource for employment (internships, part-time, or full-time) or graduate school reference letters
- Assistance in determining your major or career goals

## 4. PREPARING TO MEET WITH YOUR PROFESSOR

Professors are very busy people and their time is often limited. However, most professors do schedule regular office hours so that their students have the ability to visit with them outside of the classroom. Therefore, because your professors' time is limited, and they are providing you the opportunity to meet with them during their busy schedule, you should do everything possible to be prepared for your meeting with them. Listed below are some tips to keep in mind when you are planning to meet with your professor.

- Even if your professor holds regular office hours, contact your professor to inform them that you would like to meet with them.
- Be sure that you are not late or that you forget about your appointment. If you are not sure of where your professor's office is, locate it prior to the date of your appointment.
- If you will be late to your appointment, contact your professor as soon as possible to inform them of the situation. Always offer to reschedule the appointment if it is more convenient for them.
- Avoid meeting with your professor right after class. You will usually have a difficult time getting one-on-one time since other students may be around. In addition, your professor may not be able to concentrate on the conversation since they may need to organize their materials and rush to teach another class.
- Prior to your appointment, be sure you are familiar with the materials you have been presented in class. Also, be sure to organize the materials that you wish to discuss during your meeting. Having your course textbook and class notes available during your meeting is best.

## 5. DEALING WITH DIFFICULT PROFESSORS

Although dealing with difficult professors tends to be infrequent, you may encounter a professor that you consider to be difficult to deal with. The best advice on how to deal with a difficult professor is to avoid being negative. Negative actions, or reactions, will only escalate the situation in the wrong direction. Instead, try to implement many of the tips provided earlier in this section, such as participating in class discussions or scheduling one-on-one meetings. By taking interest in and being enthusiastic about the course materials, your professor may become easier to work with. However, if you believe the relationship between you and your professor is not productive and is directly affecting your grade in the course, contact your academic advisor or college counselor for assistance.

# SELECTING A MAJOR

Selecting a major requires time, information and commitment. Because there are no set guidelines on how to select a major, the decision involves a lot of personal choices. Although this section will not specify what major you should pursue, it will, however, provide you a guide to assist you in locating the major that best meets your needs.

## 1. WHY DO YOU SELECT A MAJOR?

A major is used as a guide to develop your class schedule, internships, and other activities during college, as well as prepare you for your career. By selecting a major, you and your academic advisor will be able to coordinate your class schedule in order to allow you to graduate in the least amount of time. In addition, selecting a major allows you to take advantage of internships and other activities during college to further expand your knowledge of the opportunities that exist for you after you complete your degree.

## 2. WHEN DO YOU SELECT A MAJOR?

The time you need to select a major varies depending on the college you are attending. Most colleges require their students to select a major in the latter part of their sophomore year or the beginning of their junior year. Be sure to visit with your academic advisor to determine the requirements that your college maintains.

Although there may seem to be a sufficient amount of time to select a major, you should not delay the process. There are a lot of decisions that will need to be made during your first year of college. However, you should not rush your decision either. Give yourself an ample opportunity to investigate all the options available to you.

## 3. HOW DO YOU SELECT A MAJOR?

There are no set guidelines on how to select a major. The decision requires time, information and commitment. This section focuses on gathering the information you will need to assist you in selecting the major that best meets your needs.

### Create A List Of Topics/Careers That Interest You

The first step you should undertake in deciding what major to choose is to make a list of the topics/careers that interest you. Feel free to add to this list as new interests develop. You will find, however, that as you begin researching and participating in the opportunities that exist within each of these areas, you will start removing certain topics/careers from your list. Continue this process as you proceed through your college career, not only to locate your major, but also to locate a career.

### Determine The Requirements For A Major

After you have compiled a list of potential majors in which you have an interest, research the requirements that you must fulfill for that major. You can locate this information in your college's course catalog or by visiting your academic advisor. Review the requirements and determine if you are capable and committed to completing them.

### Visit With People Who Work In Areas That Interest You

One of the best ways to gather information about majors that interest you is to visit with the people who are working in that field. Not only can they answer questions about their work and what it took them to get where they are, but they can also provide you information that you may not have considered. Listed below are a few ways to locate contacts within a certain major.

- Ask for assistance from your college's Career Center and Alumni departments in locating contacts. They often keep a database of their alumni's contact information, as well as their professions.
- Search the Internet and telephone book for businesses in your area and ask to visit with a person who holds the position you are interested in.

This is also a great way to make new contacts and find possible internship opportunities.

* Visit with professors who teach courses in the majors you are interested in developing a career. They often have a wealth of contacts in the business world and can direct you to some great resources.

**Take Courses That Interest You**
One of the best ways to learn about a topic that interests you is to take a course on the subject. Most colleges allow students to take courses without credit, often referred to as "auditing". Take a variety of courses to learn what interests you the most. Visit with your academic advisor about courses that are offered that provide the best review of a subject.

**Work-Study & Internships**
A good "hands-on" way to experience the opportunities available in a major is through a work-study or internship program. Visit with your school's Career Center to inquire about opportunities that are available, as well as how to participate in them. Also, review the "Education Employment" section on page 136.

**Aptitude Exam**
An aptitude exam provides you insight about your personality and skills, as well as your strengths and weaknesses. In many cases, these exams will correlate potential careers that best match the results from your exam. Many college Career Centers offer these exams to students, or can at least provide you with information on where to locate a testing facility.

## 4. CHANGING YOUR MAJOR
Selecting a major, as this section has described, is not an exact science. In some cases, after students have taken a series of courses in a major and/or experienced an internship within that major, they decide their chosen major may not be the best one for them. If you decide you need to change your major, visit with your academic advisor to determine what steps need to be taken in order to change your major. In most cases, changing your major is a fairly easy process. However, be aware that obtaining prerequisites for a new major can delay your intended graduation date. Therefore, you may want to consider other options, such as double majoring or continuing with your chosen major and adding a minor.

## 5. SELECTING A DOUBLE MAJOR OR MINOR

Graduating with two majors or a minor is a good way to get the most out of your academic experience at college, as well as improve your chances for employment. However, attempting this task is not only difficult, but also time-consuming. Be sure to consider the following tips if you are considering choosing a double major or minor.

- To minimize the amount of time you spend in college, you need to choose your second major or minor early in your college career so that you can maximize your class schedule to graduate in a timely manner.
- Because of the number of classes you will need to take in order to acquire an additional degree, your schedule may not allow you to take other elective courses that interest you.
- Choose areas of study that work well together for career opportunities. Choosing dramatically different majors or minors may cause concern with potential employers who may consider distinctly different double majors or minors as a sign of indecisiveness.
- Due to the amount of time needed to acquire a second major or minor, you must be an effective time manager. Be sure to read the "Time Management" section on page 82 for more information.

# SELECTING, SCHEDULING & REGISTERING FOR COURSES

The process of selecting, scheduling and registering for courses is an extremely important part of your college career. In order to achieve the best education possible, you should dedicate a lot of time and effort to researching each of these steps. Although there are many factors to consider when selecting, scheduling and registering for courses, this section will guide you through each of these steps by providing you various tips on how to make each process as easy and stress-free as possible.

## 1. MEET WITH YOUR ACADEMIC ADVISOR
The first step to selecting and scheduling your courses is to meet with your academic advisor. Your academic advisor is an invaluable resource for information regarding selecting and scheduling courses, as well as other information to assist you with your college career. To learn more about meeting with your academic advisor, and the information they can assist you with, refer to the "Academic Advisors" section on page 20.

## 2. CREATE YOUR GRADUATION SCHEDULE
As you begin your college course selection and scheduling process, it is important to keep your graduation schedule in mind. Your graduation schedule is an outline of all the courses you must complete, as well as the terms (semester or quarter) that each course should be completed in order for you to graduate. Be sure to review the "Selecting A Major" section on

page 51 for assistance in determining your major. If you are just starting college and have not yet chosen a major, do not worry. You will soon determine a major and can then complete your graduation schedule. When you are ready to develop a graduation schedule, the following information will assist you.

- Most college course catalogs provide students a sample graduation schedule. Use this as your starting point and adjust it to meet your specific needs. If your course catalog does not provide a sample schedule, work with your academic advisor to create one.

- Be aware of required prerequisites for courses you intend to take later in your schedule and adjust your schedule appropriately to ensure that you complete all required prerequisites early in your schedule.

- If you are unsure about the major you want to pursue, consider adding introductory courses from other subjects into your earlier terms. In most cases, your schedule will allow for an occasional elective course while still maintaining your target graduation date. If you decide later that you want to change your major, do not worry. Review the "Selecting A Major" section on page 51 for more information on how to change your major. Remember, most students change their major at least once during their college career and are still able to graduate within their intended graduation time frame.

- Be aware of courses that are offered on an irregular schedule. For example, courses that are not in high demand may only be offered every other term or year. Your course catalog should give you this information. However, you may want to visit with your academic advisor regarding courses that might have irregular schedules in order for you to adjust your graduation schedule accordingly.

- Try to develop a mix of difficult and easier courses into each term to avoid stressful situations and to assist you in maintaining a good Grade Point Average.

- Follow the college's recommended number of credit hours per term. Although taking more credits each term may allow you to graduate earlier, you may not graduate at the level of success you had intended. Also, taking fewer credit hours in a term can create a situation where you may not be able to graduate in the time period you had planned.

- Review your course catalog to determine if courses you are interested in are offered during the summer. If so, taking summer courses may allow more flexibility in your overall schedule, allowing you to possibly graduate earlier or the ability to take additional courses of interest during your college career.

## 3. REQUIRED COURSES

Regardless of your major, every college requires students to complete a specific minimum requirement of credit hours in certain subjects, such as math, English and science. These required courses are usually completed during your freshman and sophomore years in college or even while you were in high school, for example in Advanced Placement courses or while attending a college in your senior year of high school.

To determine the course level that you will be allowed to enter into, as well as the possibility that you might be able to waive certain required credit hours, students may be required to take a placement exam. The length and content of the exam varies by college, but the results are used in the same manner – to determine at what course levels you should start your college career. Your academic advisor and student handbook are great resources to use in determining the amount of required course credit hours you must complete, as well as how the placement process works.

If, after receiving your placement results, you are not satisfied with the entrance level you were assigned, some colleges will allow students the ability to "challenge" a course. "Challenging" a course usually involves requesting approval from the professor who teaches the course to allow you to take an exam that covers the materials that will be presented in the course, very much like a final exam. If you complete the exam successfully, you are not required to take the full course, but may be required to pay a fee for completing the "challenging" process and for being awarded the credits for the course. However, if you do not complete the "challenging process," not only must you pay the fee for participating in the "challenging process," but you must also pay to take the complete course. In most cases, the "challenging process" is only allowed for introductory courses.

## 4. SELECTING COURSES

College students are often provided a lot of options when it comes to selecting courses. For example, depending on your major, you may be required to complete 15 credit hours of science courses (usually 3-5 different courses). However, you may be provided 12 different courses (or over 30 credit hours) to select from in order to meet that credit hour requirement. Therefore, before you decide on the courses that you will take, it is essential that you spend time researching your options. Remember, selecting the courses you take during college is just as important as selecting your major. Listed below are a few methods to use in gathering information about your course options.

- Review your college's course catalog for descriptions of courses. In some cases, the course catalog may only provide brief descriptions of each course. If you need further details, contact the specific department office, the professor who is teaching the course, or possibly the Internet Web site for that professor or course.
- Visit with students who have already taken courses that you are considering selecting and ask their opinion of the value of the course.
- Visit with your academic advisor for their opinion of courses that will provide you the most value.
- Some colleges make publications available that provide student reviews of courses. Although this information can be a valuable resource of information, be careful, as reviews can skew the true value of a course.

## 5. SELECTING PROFESSORS

Once you have determined the courses that you want to take, you must decide which professor to take the course from. Although your selection of professors will be limited as you begin to take more advanced courses, introductory courses are often taught by a variety of professors. The following information will assist you in selecting a professor that best meets your needs.

- Often, the best way to select a professor is from word-of-mouth of fellow students. Before selecting a professor, visit with students who have taken the course from different professors and compare their evaluations.
- In some cases, introductory classes may be taught by an associate professor or teaching assistant. This does not necessarily mean the class will be less valuable. However, if you are concerned, you may want to schedule a meeting with the associate professor or teaching assistant to discuss the class in order to develop a better opinion of their teaching abilities.
- Compare the teaching and grading methods of different professors, however, do not select a professor solely on their grading procedures. In

some cases, professors with relaxed grading procedures are not always the best educators.

- Look for professors who challenge their students to learn. Although the course may be more difficult, the value of learning from such a professor will prove itself in later courses that build on the material you had learned from that professor.

- Some colleges make publications available that provide student reviews of professors. Although this information can be a valuable resource of information, be careful, as reviews can skew the true value of a professor.

## 6. REGISTRATION

Once you have researched the courses that you want to take and the professors that you want to take them from, you are ready to develop your upcoming term's course schedule and register it. This section will provide you a variety of tips on how to develop a schedule that will meet your needs, as well as how to make the registration process as easy as possible.

**Developing Your Schedule**

As you review the time schedule for the courses that you want to take for the upcoming term, be sure to consider the following tips.

- Before developing your schedule for the upcoming term, be sure to consider any time dedications you may have during that term, such as your work schedule or extracurricular activities, and plan your schedule accordingly.

- During your first few terms of college you will most likely be one of the last groups of students allowed to register for courses. Therefore, as you develop your schedule, be sure to have alternative course times available in case your first choices are not available.

- Schedule classes during the time of day when you are most alert. For example, if you are not a "morning" person, avoid scheduling early classes that you will have difficulty paying attention in, attending regularly or arriving on-time.

- Try to develop a balance in your weekly schedule, such as an equal number of classes each day versus all of your classes on only two or three days of the week. Having too many classes in one day can cause problems with your study habits and class preparation. In addition, you can create a situation where you have exams in back-to-back classes and are unable to adequately prepare for them.

- Provide yourself a break in between classes if at all possible. This will allow you time to complete your note taking from the class you just got out of and also allow you a sufficient amount of time to prepare for the next class.
- Consider the distance between class locations and travel time when scheduling your classes.

## Dealing With A Closed Course

Even with the best-planned schedule, you may occasionally experience a time when a class you want to take has already been filled prior to your registration time and is listed as a closed class. If this situation occurs, and you are unable to choose to attend any of the other times the class is offered or if it is the only class available, consider some of the options listed below.

- Visit with the professor of the closed course directly and plead your case. In some cases, a professor may limit the class size in order for the professor to maintain their workload, but may be able to allow some flexibility for special cases.
- Depending on the type of course, and if the same professor of the closed class is teaching the same course at a different time, you may be able to register for the open class, but attend the lecture of the closed class. However, you may be required to attend exam dates for the class you registered for. Be sure to visit with the professor before proceeding with this option.
- Some professors will allow students to sit-in on a closed class to fill spots that may become available as registered students drop the course. Be sure to ask the professor if there is a waiting list that you can add your name to.

## Avoiding Registration Delays

The last thing you want to happen when you are ready to register your schedule is to experience a delay. Be sure to consider these tips to avoid delaying your registration.

- Although most colleges assign registration priority on seniority, you must remember that there are a lot of other students at your seniority level. Therefore, when your seniority level registration time becomes available, do not delay. Have your schedule ready and arrive at the registration destination early.

- Visit with your academic advisor about the registration process and be sure you have all the needed information. Also check the college newspaper and website for updated information about the registration process. Last minute changes do occur occasionally.
- If your college requires your academic advisor to approve your schedule before you can register, be sure to schedule an appointment with them well in advance of the registration process to address any concerns they may have and to receive the appropriate documentation of their approval.
- Most colleges will not allow students with outstanding balances to register. Check with your college prior to the registration process to ensure all outstanding balances are paid, including fines for overdue library books, traffic fines, and unpaid fees from the previous term.
- If your college allows students to register for courses on-line, be sure you are aware of the procedures for doing so. Most colleges that offer this service may also offer a short course on how to register for course on-line. If they do, sign up for the course early to avoid delays. If you have any questions about the on-line registration process, contact the registration office immediately for clarification and/or a demonstration.

# STUDYING

Studying is an extremely important part of your time at college. Learning to study effectively and efficiently will often determine how successful you will be in college, as well as in your career after college. This section will provide you advice on how, when and where to study, as well as what to avoid when you are studying.

## 1. EFFECTIVE STUDY TIPS

### Go To Every Class

Effective studying begins by attending each of your classes. Classes are not only opportunities for your professors to discuss important topics in length, but classes are also an opportunity to ask questions, listen to other students' questions and learn what information you may need to focus more of your time on.

### Study Throughout The Term Of Your Course

Studying throughout the term of your course is an effective and efficient method of studying. A basic rule of thumb is to study at least two hours for every hour of class lecture. This is accomplished by reviewing materials before class, studying between classes, and studying after your class. By following this process, you will truly learn the material versus memorizing it.

## Study Difficult And Boring Courses First

Studying for difficult and boring courses involves the use of more energy to effectively learn the information than for an entertaining course. Therefore, you should concentrate on studying for your more difficult or boring courses first when you have more energy and can focus your full attention on studying.

## Understand The Examination Process

Prior to studying, find out as much information as you can about the examination process. For example, ask your professors if their exams will be in an essay, multiple choice, or true/false format. Also ask what materials will be covered on the exam, such as lecture materials, readings from the class text, assignments, or all class material.

## Review Previous Quizzes And Exams

In some cases, professors will offer their students old versions of class quizzes and exams as tools to help students prepare for the exam. If they do, ask to have these materials made available early in the term of the course so that you can review them and develop a proper study program for the class. In addition, visit with other students who have already taken the course and ask them for their opinion on how to best prepare for the class quizzes and exams. Also, be sure to keep all of your assignments, quizzes and exams throughout the course so that you can use them as guides when preparing for future quizzes and exams.

## Attend Review Sessions

Review sessions are a valuable resource that should be utilized when available. Professors often offer review sessions for their students prior to a quiz or exam to review important information that the students should know from previous class sessions and to answer questions that students may have about the class materials. In addition, they may provide hints/suggestions on what students can expect on the quiz or exam and how they think students should best prepare for the quiz or exam.

## Avoid Scheduling Long Study Periods

Studying for a long period of time can be counterproductive and should be avoided. Instead, schedule shorter study sessions throughout the day to avoid becoming bored and tired. If you must study for an extended length of time, incorporate short breaks to relax and rejuvenate your energy level.

**Set Goals**
Before beginning a study session, set a goal for what you want to accomplish during that session, such as reading the next day's class materials, reviewing the previous day's notes, or creating a study chart. More often than not, you will have a large amount of information to study and by setting goals you will avoid feeling overwhelmed.

**Understand Your Body**
People tend to have a certain time period during the day when they are the most active or their bodies have the most energy, hence the terms a "morning-person" or a "night owl." If you are more active during a certain time period of the day, utilize this time for studying. By doing so, you will spend less time learning the same amount of information than you would have if you had studied during a period of time when your body is less active.

**Focus On The Big Picture**
Most courses are taught in steps to eventually get to a certain outcome. For example, in an introductory accounting course you will learn several small steps, such as why accounting is important and how to develop a balance sheet and an income statement. Eventually, you will take all the steps you were taught to get to the "big picture," which for an introductory accounting course is to be able to create and read a financial report. By focusing on what the "big picture" of a class is, you will be better able to understand the class materials as you proceed through and study for the course.

## 2. WHEN TO STUDY?
As mentioned in a few of the study tips above, determining the best time to study is a personal preference. However, there are some general guidelines to keep in mind when developing an effective study program.

**Study Before Class**
Attending a class unprepared is a wasted opportunity. By completing assigned readings and assignments prior to class, you will not only be able to better understand the lecture as it is being presented, but you will also be able to participate in the lecture by asking educated questions which will allow you to learn the information more quickly and study more effectively.

**Study Between Classes**
Schedules for college students usually involve taking several courses each term. Rarely will all of these courses be offered back-to-back. Studying between classes is a great use of this time, particularly since colleges tend to offer students ample locations for studying on campus. In addition, studying between classes breaks up your study time and minimizes the need for longer study periods, thus creating an effective study program. When studying between classes, try using this time to prepare for your next class lecture or to take notes and/or complete an assignment for the class that you have just completed.

**Study After Classes**
Taking time to review your notes after completing a class is an effective method of studying. Because the lecture is fresh in your mind, you will be able to add additional information to your notes that will help you when studying at a later time. Consider using the time after class to rewrite/reorganize your notes or to develop a summary outline listing information that you believe you need to focus more time on as well as information you believe to be important.

## 3. WHERE TO STUDY?
Finding a good location to study is just as important to the studying process as how to study and what materials to study. The following tips will assist you in creating an effective and productive study area.
- Locate an area with sufficient temperature control and lighting.
- Create a study area that is comfortable, but not too comfortable. For example, do not create your study area on a couch or bed. These areas will encourage rest and relaxation versus activity and concentration.
- Keep your study area free of distractions, such as a telephone, television, or radio. Even having your study area located near a window that provides a view may be distracting to some people.
- Avoid cluttering your study area by keeping your study materials organized.

## 4. STUDY GROUPS

Studying with a group of fellow students offers a number of benefits. However, study groups can also be ineffective unless the group is dedicated to working together to learn the subject matter and not simply getting together to socialize. This section will discuss the benefits of participating in a study group as well as how to organize/coordinate your own study group.

### Benefits Of Studying In A Study Group
Listed below are the primary benefits of studying in a group.
- Offers participants a gauge of how well they really understand the subject matter.
- Provides participants the opportunity to clarify areas of the subject matter that they do not understand.
- Encourages participants to share views and perspectives that often broaden each of the participant's level of understanding.
- Allows participants an opportunity to share class notes, quiz one another, and develop studying strategies.

### Forming A Study Group
In order to form an effective study group, several important factors need to be considered. One of the best ways to find participants for a study group is to visit with other students that share your interest in learning more about the course. Listed below are a few factors to keep in mind.
- Develop a group with diverse backgrounds and strengths to bring a wide range of perspectives to the group.
- Coordinate a group of participants that have the ability to meet on a regular schedule and at a time that meets everyone's needs.
- Set ground rules as to what is expected from the participants, such as setting a schedule of the topics to be discussed at each meeting and requiring each participant to prepare for the meetings by studying the material.

## 5. COMMON STUDY PROBLEMS

There are numerous reasons students do not study. Listed on the next page are a few of the most common reasons. These are provided so that you can avoid falling into these situations and can instead develop a study program to keep them from happening to you.

- Delaying studying because you believe there will be a sufficient amount of time to study later in the week, month or class term
- Believing that there is way too much material to study and that there is not enough time to study all of it
- Wasting time by studying improperly
- Not spending enough time studying.
- Studying in a poor location
- Believing that by studying for an exam right before you take the exam the information will be recalled easily
- Believing that because the class is boring or appears to be unimportant, studying the materials is a waste of time
- Falling asleep while studying

## 6. STUDY ASSISTANCE

If you are having difficulty in a class or in developing a study program, there are several options available to assist you to correct your problem. Listed below are a few options to consider.

- Contact your professor or school counselor and ask them to assist you, or request suggestions on where you can obtain assistance.
- Obtain a tutor. In some cases, colleges provide tutors at no charge. However, if your college does not, consider hiring a tutor for a few tutoring sessions to see if the expense is worth the cost.
- Sign up for a general course on studying through your college. If your college does not offer a course on studying, consider taking the course from a learning center or professional test-preparation company.

# TAKING EXAMS

College exams are very different from exams taken during high school. Although they do not tend to be fun, they are a key component of your college experience. The difficulty and format of college exams will vary depending on the college that you attend, the professor who is teaching the course, as well as the class you are taking. The timing of exams also varies. Exams can occur every time class meets, once a month, or even once a term. In college, exams usually encompass a large portion, if not all, of your final grade. Therefore, doing well on exams is essential to a successful college experience. This section provides you with helpful advice and strategies to be successful on your college exams.

## 1. STRATEGIES FOR TAKING AN EXAM
The following tips will assist you in taking an exam successfully.

### Relax And Maintain A Positive Attitude
When you receive an exam, take a deep breath and convince yourself that you will do well on the exam. Staying calm during an exam will allow you to concentrate, stay focused, and obtain positive results.

### Be Comfortable
Being comfortable during an exam is essential. If you are too hot or too cold, you may not be able to focus your full attention on the exam. Therefore, try wearing layered clothing so that you can adjust to a temperature that makes you the most comfortable.

## Preview The Exam
When you receive your exam, take a few moments to preview it. This will allow you to determine the amount of time you should allocate to each section of the exam in order to complete it in the allotted time.

## Read The Instructions
Many of us have heard the story about the professor that instructed her students to read all the instructions thoroughly before beginning the exam. In that story, the professor told her students to put their names on the last page of the exam and then turn it in to her. None of the students read the instructions; they then completed the test, turned it in to her, and then all failed the exam because they did not follow her instructions. Although this is an extreme example, it does stress the importance of reading the instructions thoroughly to avoid making costly mistakes

## Complete Questions That You Know The Answers To First
After previewing your exam, mark the questions that you are confident you know the answers to. Then return to these questions and complete them first. Not only will this build up your confidence level, but it will also ensure that you do not spend too much time on questions you are unsure about or may answer incorrectly, as well as leave you little time to complete the questions you do know the answers to.

## Keep Your Work Legible
Spend the extra time on your exam to make your work legible. Often, if a professor has difficulty reading your answers, they may mark your answer as incorrect or only give you partial credit.

## Show Your Work
Be sure to provide your professor any calculations or steps that you performed to arrive at your answer. That way, when the professor is correcting the exam, they can follow the thought process you took to develop your answer. In some cases, even if your final answer is incorrect, the professor may give you partial credit for taking the correct steps.

## Concentrate During The Exam
Being distracted can cause you to do poorly on an exam. Since you are only allocated a set amount of time to complete an exam, avoid any situations or

outside distractions that may cause you to not be completely focused. If you are being distracted, take the actions necessary to stop them, such as moving to a different area of the room or informing your professor about the distraction.

## Do Not Panic If You Are Unprepared For A Question

No matter how prepared you may be for an exam, there will be times when you come to a question whose answer you are unsure of. If this situation arises, skip that question and move on to questions that you know you are prepared for. When you return to that question, develop an answer utilizing the information that you do know. Remember, some professors will allow you to earn some credit for partially correct answers.

## Learn From The Exam As You Take It

On many exams, questions often build on one another. Therefore, if you do not know the answer to a certain question, answering questions you know may assist you in developing an answer to the question that you were uncertain about.

## Set Aside Time At The End Of The Exam

If possible, try to allow yourself some additional time to review your exam after you complete it. This will provide you an opportunity to review your answers for mistakes, as well as ensure that you did not leave any questions unanswered.

## Hand In Your Exam When Time Is Called

Professors provide a set amount of time to take an exam so that all of their students are treated fairly by having an equal amount of time to answer the questions. Therefore, when the exam time expires, be sure to turn in your exam immediately as some professors may not accept late exams. However, do not be afraid to request additional time if needed.

## 2. DEALING WITH EXAM ANXIETY

Exams are often a key component to your final grade for a course, so having anxiety about an exam is natural. However, the following tips can minimize that anxiety.

- Schedule an appointment with your professor at least a week prior to the exam to discuss the exam and answer questions about materials that you are uncertain about.

- Provide yourself sufficient time to prepare for the exam.
- Arrive at the exam location early to find a comfortable location and prepare any materials that you may need during the exam.
- Avoid sitting near other students who may cause you to be distracted.
- Avoid quizzing other students and being quizzed just prior to the exam, as this may add additional stress.
- Anxiety can be reduced with a proper diet and exercise. Refer to the "Healthy Living" section on page 100 for more information.
- Maintain a positive attitude about the exam and your grade. If you prepared properly, you should do well on the exam.

## 3. CRAMMING FOR AN EXAM

Cramming for an exam is not an ideal situation and should be avoided if at all possible. However, if you do find yourself in this situation, these tips may be of some assistance.

- Try to maintain a positive attitude. If you attended class and have read the materials, you should do fine on the exam even if you did not have a sufficient amount of time to study.
- Use whatever time you do have to prepare for the exam as efficiently as possible, such as focusing on materials you are unfamiliar with instead of reviewing the materials that you know well.
- Take frequent, but short breaks, such as once an hour, to stretch and take a short walk. This will keep you active and awake.
- Avoid studying on your bed, couch or other location that can cause you to be distracted or cause you to become sleepy. Find a location that is well lit and comfortable.
- Avoid the use of stimulants such as coffee, soda or over-the-counter drugs. Although stimulants may keep you active while studying, the after-effects can cause you to be extremely drowsy and/or cause your heart rate to increase significantly, which can be counterproductive during an exam.
- Eat healthy foods while studying and just prior to the exam. Junk food provides limited nutrients and offers little energy to help you concentrate on your exam.
- Try to get a sufficient amount of rest prior to the exam so that you can think clearly.

## 4. THE NIGHT BEFORE & DAY OF THE EXAM

The time period immediately before an exam (night before & day of the exam) is when students often make their biggest mistakes. To be prepared for an exam and be at your peak performance, try implementing some of the following tips.

- Maintain a regular diet and sleep schedule. Staying up late the night before your exam or sleeping in late the morning of your exam can cause your mind to work less effectively. In addition, an unhealthy diet can also cause you not to perform as well as you could. See the "Healthy Living" section on page 100 for more information.
- Give yourself a sufficient amount of time prior to the exam to gather needed materials. If you are rushed, you may forget something important. One suggestion to avoid being rushed is gathering important items the night before. That way, if you cannot locate something that you will need, you have an opportunity to find replacements.
- Taking a shower before your exam will help stimulate your body and keep your mind focused on the exam.
- If allowed, bring a small snack and/or drink to your exam, such as a nutrient bar/drink. Not only will these items keep you from being distracted by hunger or thirst, but they will also provide you a healthy form of energy throughout the exam.
- Glance through material the morning of the exam, to refresh your mind, especially if the test is a fill-in-the-blank exam.

## 5. TAKING DIFFERENT TYPES OF EXAMS

College professors offer a variety of exam formats in order to find the best method to test their students on the materials they taught as well for ease of grading. This section provides tips on how to successfully take some of the more common forms of exams.

### Essay Exams

- Read all the questions thoroughly before starting and answer questions that you feel the most comfortable with first.
- Before you write your answer, make a quick outline of key points you want to discuss in your answer.
- Try to provide a quick summary of the answer to the question in the first sentence of your essay. If you take too long to develop an answer to an

essay question, your professor may not feel that you fully understand the topic and may only give you partial credit.

- Write legibly. If your professor cannot read your writing, they may not provide you with any credit for your work.
- Try to incorporate as much relevant information into your answers as possible.
- Leave extra space between the paragraphs of your answer. This will provide you room to add additional information to your answer later.
- If you are running short of time, outline key points of your answer. Although your answer may not be in essay form, your professor may provide you partial credit.
- If possible, leave extra space around the margins of your answer in order to add additional information later if needed. In addition, this space will provide your professor adequate space for comments.

**True/False Exams**
- Read all of the exam's questions before you begin. Answer those statements you know the answers to first, then return to the remaining statements. By answering statements you know the answers to first, you may be able to develop answers to other statements that you were previously unsure about.
- A common trick used in true and false exams is to add negatives to a sentence in order to confuse the reader. For example, consider these two versions of a true or false statement.
  *"It is not always true that all birds use their wings to fly."*
  *"All birds always use their wings to fly."*
  Although the answer to both of these questions is false, the first one is written in a way to try to confuse the reader.
- Every part of a true statement must be true. If any part of the statement is in question, it is false.
- Watch out for key words or qualifiers such as "all," "most," "sometimes," "never," or "rarely." Although the answer to a statement may appear to be true, the addition of one of these key words or qualifiers can change the meaning all together and make it a false statement.
- If you have to provide an explanation to a statement to make it true, the statement is false.

**Multiple-Choice Exams**
- Read all the questions thoroughly before starting and answer the questions that you know the answers to first. By answering the questions you know the answers to first, you may be able to gather information from these questions to help you answer questions that you were previously unsure about.
- A common practice in multiple-choice exams is to have several similar answers available for you to choose from. Therefore, as you read a question, anticipate the answer before reviewing the available choice of answers. This will help you from being misled or from doubting your initial answer.
- If you are unsure of the answer to a question, read over all of the answers that are provided. Cross-out those that you are certain are incorrect and try to develop your answer from the choices that remain.
- In some cases, professors may enforce a steeper penalty for answering a multiple-choice question incorrectly. If this is the case for your exam, and you are uncertain as to what the correct answer is, it may not be worth the risk of answering that question.

**Open Book/Open Note Exams**
Open book/open note exams are often the hardest exams to take. Because you have access to the information to check your answers, students often do not prepare for these exams as diligently as they would for other exams. Students also waste large amounts of time confirming answers to questions they already know the answers to. These tips will help you maximize the use of your book and notes during an open book/open note exam.
- Study for open book/open note exams as you would if you did not have access to your study materials.
- Before the exam, place tabs on important pages of the textbook, lecture notes, and class assignments, particularly the areas that you have difficulty understanding. This will help you to avoid wasting time searching for that information during the exam.
- Read all the questions thoroughly before starting and answer questions that you know the answers to first. Avoid confirming your answers to these questions by reviewing your study materials until you have answered all of your other questions.
- When answering a question you are unsure about, try to develop an answer first and then use your book and notes to confirm your answer.

- Be sure your answers are written legibly and that you provide sufficient space in your answers to add additional information to them later if time allows.

## Take Home Exams

As with open book/open note exams, students often fail to study sufficiently for take home exams. These tips will help you successfully complete a take home exam.

- Study for take home exams as you would for any other type of exam.
- Prepare for the exam by organizing all your study materials, such as your notes, textbook, and homework assignments.
- Review the exam thoroughly before leaving the classroom. If you have any questions, ask your professor at that time. Also ask if, and how, the professor can be contacted if you have additional questions that you may need answered at a later time.
- Answer questions that you are most comfortable with first and then move to the more difficult questions later.
- Because take home exams offer the luxury of time, professors often have a higher standard of grading for this type of exam. Therefore, be sure to develop strong answers by using all the information you have available.
- Before you write your final answer, make an outline of the key points you want to discuss in your answer.
- Try to provide a quick summary of the answer to the question in the first sentence.
- If you are not able to use a computer to answer questions, be sure to write legibly.

## Oral Exams

Oral exams are often only used during graduate school; however, there are instances when undergraduates may need to take an oral exam. These tips will help you take an oral exam successfully.

- Visit with your professor about how the oral exam will be conducted and prepare for the exam by conducting "mock" oral exams with a colleague.
- Dress and act professionally during the exam.
- Arrive at the exam location early. This will help you relax and stay focused, as well as avoid making your professor wait for you to arrive.

- Before answering a question, take a few moments to think out your answer.
- If you need more time to think out your answer or are unsure about the question, ask for the question to be repeated or ask for additional information.
- Summarize your answer in your first sentence and then continue with subsequent sentences that develop your answer.
- Avoid rambling if you do not know the answer to a question. Try to develop key points with the information you know as you may be awarded partial credit for an answer.
- Avoid answering questions with one-word answers. Oral exams are given to determine your true knowledge of a topic, not how quickly you can provide an answer.
- Avoid annoying speech mannerisms such as "um," "you know," "you know what I mean," "like," etc.

## 6. BEFORE TURNING IN YOUR EXAM

Some of the most common mistakes made on exams are often the easiest to avoid. To help you avoid these mistakes, be sure to follow these steps before turning in your exam.

- Make sure your name, student identification number, and other required information are on your exam.
- If you are providing answers to your exam on a Scantron / bubble form, be sure to double check that you filled in the correct bubble for each question
- Review the exam instructions one final time to ensure that you have fulfilled all the requirements.

## 7. REVIEWING YOUR GRADED EXAM

Reviewing your graded exam is important for a number of reasons. Not only can reviewing your exam help you catch mistakes that may have been made during the grading process, but it will also help you understand any mistakes you may have made on the exam. The following tips will help you effectively review your exam.

- Calculate your score to ensure that the grader added up your score correctly.

- Review the exam to locate questions that may have been written unclearly or that could have been answered with multiple responses. If you locate a question like this, address the situation with your professor to determine if your answer to the question can be reconsidered.
- Determine where the questions on the exam originated from, such as from the professor's lecture, course textbook, or homework assignments. This may assist you in studying for future exams with that professor.
- Correct each of the incorrect and partially correct answers you provided on the exam to better understand why your answer was wrong and what information you were missing. This will help you better understand the class materials and help prepare you for any mid-term or final exams.
- Schedule an appointment with your professor to discuss any questions that you may have, as well as to ask for their advice on studying for future exams.

# TEXTBOOKS

Almost every college course you take will have at least one required textbook associated with the course. Many textbooks can be intimidating at first glance; however, if they are understood and used correctly, textbooks can be extremely valuable. This section will assist you in understanding how textbooks are used in college, how you can read and study textbooks effectively, as well as tips on buying and selling your textbooks.

## 1. HOW ARE TEXTBOOKS USED?

Although almost every college course has at least one required textbook for the course, not all college courses use them in the same manner. In fact, in some situations, you may find that the textbook is rarely, if ever, used as a key component of the course. Listed below are a few methods of how professors commonly use textbooks as part of the course.

### Textbooks As An Integral Part Of The Course

In some cases, if a professor believes the textbook is written well, they will use it as an integral part of their course. In fact, they will often build the course syllabus around the content of the textbook. If this is the case for your course, be sure to read and study your textbook effectively as materials for course assignments and exams will often come directly from your textbook. Math and science courses are good examples of courses where textbooks are an integral part of the course.

### Textbooks As A Course Supplement

A more popular method of how textbooks are used in college courses is as a course supplement. Professors who use textbooks in this manner will use the textbook as a way to reinforce important topics or to prepare students for lecture discussions. When textbooks are used in this manner, assignments and exam questions are often developed from the lecture and the textbook.

**Textbooks As Suggested Reading**
In less frequent situations, professors may list a textbook as required reading material for the course, but never utilize the materials from the textbook in the course lecture, assignments or exams. Professors may utilize textbooks in this manner because they believe doing so will assist the student with understanding the materials that are being presented during the lecture portion of the course.

## 2. READING YOUR TEXTBOOKS
Textbooks are used for a number of reasons including preparing you for the class lecture, studying for an exam, expanding your knowledge base, and completing assignments. In order to accomplish these tasks, you must be able to read your textbooks effectively. Listed below are some tips on how to become an effective reader.

**Schedule Time**
Reading a textbook effectively takes time and commitment. Therefore you need to schedule a sufficient amount of time into your daily/weekly schedule in order to be properly prepared for class. In addition, you need to schedule your reading time when you are the most active and can focus your attention. You may find it helpful to review the "Time Management" section on page 82 for more information about developing a schedule.

**Concentrate**
Concentration is essential to reading and understanding the materials presented in a textbook. Therefore, find a location for reading that will provide you with an environment where you can concentrate and avoid interruptions, such as the library or your bedroom. Also, avoid reading for long periods of time or reading when you are tired. Remember, the more active and aware you are, the better your concentration will be.

**Maintain A Positive Attitude**
If you believe that reading a textbook for your course is a waste of your time, then it probably will be. Instead, focus on the positive aspects of reading the textbook, such as doing well in the course, expanding your

knowledge about the topic or how the course will help you obtain the job you have always wanted.

### Preview The Information
Before you begin reading your textbook, take a few minutes to review all of the information that you are expected to read before the next class session. This will allow you to know how the information will be presented to you and what amount of time you will need to schedule in order to read the information effectively.

### Find The Main Point
Textbooks are written in a format that provides the reader information in sequence to develop a main point. Therefore, as you read your assigned information, be aware of the main points as they develop and remember them. You may need to review the information several times in order to locate the main point. Compare the main point(s) that you had gathered to those provided in the chapter summary. If your textbook does not have a chapter summary, compare your results with those of your classmates.

## 3. STUDYING YOUR TEXTBOOKS
Studying your textbook is just as important, if not more, than reading it. The studying process should take place after you have completed the tasks mentioned in the "Reading Your Textbooks" section above. Listed below are some tips on studying your textbook. In addition, you may find it helpful to review the "Note Taking" section on page 39 for further information.

### Marking/Highlighting Your Textbook
After you have read your assigned reading and begin to study the information, mark or highlight information you believe to be important. Marking and highlighting important information will assist you in implementing this information into your class notes after you have attended the class lecture on the materials. In addition, marking and highlighting will allow you to find information within your textbook quickly. As you mark or highlight, try to develop some consistency. For example, underline definitions and highlight important topics. If the information you are studying contains a large number of formulas or definitions, you may find it helpful to write these out on a separate sheet of paper for easier review.

**Adding Textbook Information Into Your Study Materials**
You may find it helpful, when studying, to add important information from your textbook into your other study materials. Not only is this a great way to learn the materials, but it will also help you understand how all the class materials relate. For example, when reviewing your class lecture notes, refer to your textbook and add related information from your textbook to your notes. This will help you clarify information that you may not have completely understood from either the lecture or the textbook.

Another helpful method of using information from your textbook in your study materials, and a great way to avoid mistakes in the grading process, is to place page numbers from the textbook into the answers of your assignments that assisted you in answering the question. For example, when answering a question you might start your answer out like this: "As mentioned on page 45, paragraph 2 of our textbook, the author states that ___." You can use a similar format to this when reviewing your exams. Place relevant page numbers from your textbook next to the question on your exam that it relates to. This will help you learn where you may have made mistakes, assist you in defending your answer to your professor if you believe your answer was incorrectly graded, and will assist you in recalling information when preparing for your final exam.

## 4. BUYING & SELLING YOUR TEXTBOOKS
Textbooks can be very expensive and usually make up a significant portion of your college related expenses each term. To help reduce the expense of your textbooks and to assist in recovering some of that expense at the end of the term, consider some of these tips.

- Purchase used textbooks. Often there is a limited supply of used textbooks from previous terms. Therefore, try to purchase your textbooks early to get the best deals.
- Buy and sell your textbooks on-line. Web-based companies are quickly entering the new and used textbook sales market, and although their selections tend to be limited, the savings can be significant.
- Sell your textbooks to other students for slightly more than the price that the bookstore will purchase it back from you.
- Before selling your textbook, consider if the textbook may be helpful for future classes you may take. If so, keeping your textbook may be more valuable to you than if you sell it.

# TIME MANAGEMENT

A challenge that many college students face is the responsibility to manage their time. Unlike high school, the classes you take, as well as when you take classes, and what you do with your time outside of class are solely your responsibility. Effectively managing your time has a direct correlation on your success in college and beyond. This section will provide you with advice on how to develop an effective schedule.

## 1. TRACKING YOUR TIME

Just like managing your money, effective time management begins by understanding how it is spent. You can accomplish this by developing a chart that includes your normal daily activities and listing the time it takes to complete each activity. A sample time-tracking chart has been provided below. Make a similar chart that contains your normal schedule for each day of the week. To help complete your chart, a few common uses of time are listed on the page following this chart.

| DAY: | Tuesday | | | |
|---|---|---|---|---|
| | **Activity** | | | **Activity** |
| **Midnight** | Sleep | | **NOON** | Go home/Eat lunch |
| **1:00 AM** | Sleep | | **1:00 PM** | Watch TV/Check E-mail |
| **2:00 AM** | Sleep | | **2:00 PM** | Study |
| **3:00 AM** | Sleep | | **3:00 PM** | Work |
| **4:00 AM** | Sleep | | **4:00 PM** | Work |
| **5:00 AM** | Sleep | | **5:00 PM** | Work |
| **6:00 AM** | Sleep | | **6:00 PM** | Eat dinner/Watch TV |
| **7:00 AM** | Wake up/Go to gym | | **7:00 PM** | Biology 300 Lab |
| **8:00 AM** | Work out/Eat breakfast/Get ready | | **8:00 PM** | Biology 300 Lab |
| **9:00 AM** | Psychology 101 | | **9:00 PM** | Study |
| **10:00 AM** | Study | | **10:00 PM** | Study |
| **11:00 AM** | English 150 | | **11:00 PM** | Watch TV/Check E-mail/Sleep |

**Common Uses Of Time:**

- Showering, grooming, & dressing
- Cooking & eating
- Studying
- Doing laundry & shopping
- Watching television
- Exercising & playing sports

- Sleeping
- Attending class
- Commuting
- Working
- Using the Internet or phone
- Spending time with friends

Once you have completed the charts containing your schedule for a normal week, calculate the time you spend on each activity during the entire week. A sample chart is provided below.

| DAY: Tuesday | |
|---|---|
| **Activity** | **Total Time Allocated To Each Activity** |
| Sleep | 7.5 hours |
| Working out at gym | 1.0 hour |
| Eating | 1.5 hours |
| Getting ready | 0.5 hours |
| Attending class | 4.0 hours |
| Studying | 4.0 hours |
| Watching TV | 1.5 hours |
| Checking Email | 1.0 hour |
| Working | 3.0 hours |
| Totals | 24.0 hours |

After calculating how you currently utilize your time, be sure to keep your time usage in mind as you proceed through this section. You may be surprised to find out that your current schedule might not necessarily meet your needs.

## 2. ACCOMPLISHING YOUR GOALS

A key component to properly managing your time is being able to accomplish your goals. The first step to accomplishing your goals is having goals to accomplish. Refer to the "Goals" section on page 28 to learn how to establish your goals. Once you have established the goals you want to accomplish, you need to develop the steps that you must take to accomplish them, as well as to create the time frame in which they need to be accomplished. An effective method of doing this is to split your goals up into long- and short-term goals. By doing so, you can easily incorporate your goals' schedule into your time management schedule.

For example, a long-term goal may be to receive no less than a 3.5 cumulative GPA during your freshman year in college. To accomplish this long-term goal, you establish several smaller short-term goals, such as developing weekly study groups, spending at least 2 hours studying for each class hour that you attend, and scheduling one-on-one meetings with all your professors at least every 3 weeks to discuss your progress and understanding of the courses. By understanding what is needed to accomplish your 3.5 cumulative GPA, you then add time to your daily and weekly schedules to allow for the study group meetings, additional study time, and meetings with your professors.

## 3. OUTLINING TIME REQUIREMENTS

Although you are ultimately responsible for how you plan your schedule, there are situations where your schedule is planned for you, such as your work schedule, final-exam schedule, and assignment-due dates. When developing your time management schedule, you need to be aware of these various time requirements in order to plan your schedule properly. An effective method of outlining your time requirements is to create a weekly, monthly, college-term and yearly schedule that designates these requirements on them. By doing so, you are continually reminded of these upcoming events and their time requirements, as you plan your time management schedule.

**Common Time Requirements:**
- Regular and final exams
- Work schedule
- Extracurricular activities
- Assignment-due dates
- Holidays and vacations
- Visitors

## 4. LIFESTYLE CONSIDERATIONS

Maintaining a balanced lifestyle is another important factor to consider when developing your time management schedule. College students often make the mistake of focusing a majority of their time on one aspect of their college experience, such as education or social activities. To get the most of your college experience, as well as maintain a healthy lifestyle, be sure to incorporate the following activities into your time management schedule.

- Academic activities, such as attending class, studying and reading
- Physical activities, such as exercise, proper nutrition and sufficient sleep
- Social activities, such as going to the movies or on a date
- Career activities, such as work-study or an internship experience
- Cultural activities, such as attending plays or speeches
- Emotional activities, such as attending church services

## 5. TIME MANAGEMENT OBSTACLES

Even the best developed plans run into an occasional problem, and time management schedules are no different. Obstacles can occur at any time and can include many different situations, but the important point to keep in mind is that your time management schedule is an evolving plan and adjustments will need to be made to meet your goals. The worst thing you can do is to stop following your schedule when an obstacle occurs. This will just cause you to become further off schedule and make it more difficult to accomplish your goals.

Listed below are some common time management obstacles that you may experience. By accepting the fact that these or other obstacles will occur, and understanding that you can adjust your schedule to accommodate them when they do occur, you will be better prepared to develop an effective and adjustable time management schedule.

**Common Time Management Obstacles:**

- Visitors
- Illness
- Procrastination
- Longer than normal commute
- Change in your work schedule

- Telephone calls
- Over-scheduling
- Extracurricular activities
- Relationships
- Boredom

## 6. DEVELOPING AN EFFECTIVE SCHEDULE

As mentioned above, developing an effective schedule is an evolving task requiring constant change. By understanding your goals, time requirements and lifestyle needs, as well as accepting the fact that obstacles do occur, you can develop an effective time management schedule. Listed below are a few tips and suggestions to assist you in developing your personal time management schedule.

**Have The Correct Tools**
When you cook a meal, the finished product is only as good as the ingredients that are used. This same concept applies to developing an effective time management schedule. Below are some tools that you should consider using when developing your time management schedule.

- *Desk/Wall Calendar* – These are great for outlining your long-term goals and time requirement activities. Try finding a desk/wall calendar that provides sufficient space for writing-out details and that allow you to view several months with ease.

- *Daily Planners* – These come in a variety of formats, including paper and electronic versions. You should pick the style that best meets your needs and that can be taken with you during the day in order to make adjustments as needed. There are also versions available that offer options to help you keep track of your daily finances.

- *Scheduling Programs For Your Computer* – There are a number of scheduling programs available on the market. Because of the diversity and expense of these programs, try developing a paper program that meets your needs first and then locate a software program that offers similar options.

**Outline Your Schedule**
The first, and often the most difficult, step in creating your time management schedule is to develop an outline. The steps listed below will assist you in developing an outline.

- *Place Time Requirement Activities On Your Desk/Wall Calendar* – Write in the dates of assignment-due dates, exam schedules, extracurricular activities and vacations.

- *Take One Week At A Time* – Once you have listed all of your time requirement activities on your desk/wall calendar, start developing your upcoming weeks' schedule *(You may find that using the time-tracking chart on page 83 helpful)*. List all the activities that occur at a set time, such as your class and work schedules. Evaluate the remaining time and start filling in these areas with activities you need to accomplish in order to meet your goals and lifestyle needs, such as study group meetings, personal study time, working-out, etc. Once you have completed your schedule, transfer the information to your daily planner. You may find it beneficial to schedule a specific day each week to outlining the upcoming weeks' schedule, such as on a Friday afternoon or Sunday morning.

**Re-Evaluate Your Schedule**
As mentioned before, even the best-developed plans need to be changed occasionally. To effectively manage your time schedule, re-evaluate your weekly schedule every day or when unplanned events occur. This will help minimize the frustration that can occur when unplanned events take place and will also allow you to continue accomplishing your goals and lifestyle needs.

**Complete Multiple Tasks At One Time**
There are several tasks that can be completed at one time, such as doing your laundry and studying. Be sure to consider these types of tasks within your schedule and plan them accordingly so that you can maximize the limited amount of time you have available.

**Be Realistic**
When developing your schedule, it is important to be realistic. Avoid planning too many activities to accomplish in one day or a week and avoid creating a schedule that is unhealthy, such as only allowing for a few hours of sleep each night. Your time at college is supposed to be one of your best experiences in life, not one that is dreaded.

# YOUR COLLEGE LIFE

## CHAPTERS

# CAMPUS ACTIVITIES

Getting involved in campus activities, other than your college courses, offers many benefits, socially and professionally. This section discusses these benefits and the variety of campus activities that are offered, as well as a few concerns you should be aware of before participating in a new campus activity.

## 1. REASONS TO GET INVOLVED IN CAMPUS ACTIVITES

There are many reasons students decide to participate in campus activities. Listed below are a few of the more common reasons.

- Assists in the transition to your new environment at college and minimizes homesickness
- Helps you to have fun and enjoy yourself
- Helps you to meet new people and make new friends
- Increases your interaction with faculty and staff members
- Develops your leadership skills
- Helps you to learn to efficiently manage your time
- Develops your "people skills"
- Helps you to learn the value of working as part of a team
- Strengthens your resume

## 2. TYPES OF CAMPUS ACTIVITIES

Every college offers a variety of campus activities for their students. Listed below are some of the more common campus activities available.

- Intercollegiate and/or intramural sports
- Student government
- Academic oriented clubs, such as the Spanish or Horticulture Club
- The student newspaper, radio or television programs
- Special interest groups, such as the Political Club
- Tutoring or counseling for students
- Greek fraternity or sorority
- On-campus religious organizations

## 3. HOW TO GET INVOLVED IN CAMPUS ACTIVITIES

As you can imagine, there are many campus activities to choose from. However, if you are like most college students, you will have a limited amount of time to participate in all of the activities that interest you. Therefore, before getting involved in a new campus activity, be sure to consider the following questions.

**Why Do You Want To Participate?**
Deciding what you want from a campus activity is just as important as picking the campus activity in which to participate. Developing new skills, networking with new people, and expanding your horizons are all good reasons to participate in a new campus activity. Therefore, before researching activities to participate in, be sure to completely understand what you are looking for and why. Knowing this will make locating campus activities that meet your needs a lot easier.

**Does The Campus Activity Meet Your Needs?**
The best way to determine if a campus activity meets your needs is to conduct some research. You can perform research in a number of ways. Listed below are just a few examples of how to accomplish this task.

- Visit with your academic advisor about campus activities that might interest you.
- If your college has a Campus Activities Center, be sure to visit with the staff and have them offer ideas and suggestions.

- Read your campus newspaper or search your college's web site to learn about active organizations and their meeting times.
- Many colleges have organizational interest fairs early in the school year to educate students about all the different activities there are to choose from. Take advantage of this situation and visit with volunteers from the organizations that you are interested in participating.

### What Requirements Are Needed To Participate?
Many campus activities require potential members to meet certain requirements before being allowed to participate. Requirements can vary from initiation fees, minimum participation requirements, or even completing a specified task. Therefore, before deciding on a specific campus activity to participate in, be sure to ask what will be required of you as a member.

## 4. GETTING THE MOST FROM CAMPUS ACTIVITIES
Campus activities are like most activities in life – you will only get out of it what you put into it. Thus, the more active you are, the more beneficial the activity will be for you. Below are a few ways to become more active in campus activities.

- Be open-minded and participate in campus activities that are different from anything that you have done in the past.
- Try to get appointed to a leadership position.
- If there are no campus activities that meet your needs, start your own.

## 5. CAMPUS ACTIVITY CONCERNS
Below are a few items to be concerned about, as you become more involved in campus activities.

- Avoid signing up for campus activities, or taking a role in a campus activity that may cause your education to suffer. Remember that your primary reason for going to college is to obtain an education.
- Never sign-up for campus activities with the intention of only building-up your resume. You never know if a potential employer will quiz you on your level of participation or knowledge of the campus activity.
- Be careful not to sign up for an activity that is beyond your financial resources.

# GREEK LIFE

Many college campuses include a Greek system that is made up of fraternities (male organizations) and sororities (female organizations). These organizations include members who share common rituals, brotherhood and goals. In addition, these organizations also have some element of secrecy in their design. This section will describe the advantages and disadvantages of Greek life, how Greek life differs from dorm life, and how to get involved in the Greek system. Finally, this section also includes common terms that are used within the Greek system.

## 1. ADVANTAGES & DISADVANTAGES OF GREEK LIFE

The Greek system was developed to provide participants a unique and rewarding experience during college. The system has many advantages; however, there are also some disadvantages. Provided below are a few of the advantages and disadvantages to be aware of before deciding to participate, or not to participate, in the Greek system.

**Advantages**
- Develop friendships that can last a lifetime
- Strengthen your skills by organizing and leading various events and/or activities
- Participate in exciting activities, such as formals, Greek Week and intramural sports
- Exposure to a vast network of contacts for career and other various opportunities through the chapter's alumni

**Disadvantages**
- Time spent focusing on academics may diminish due to commitments to other activities.
- Rushing can be disappointing, frustrating and stressful.

- Participating in required activities that you may not have an interest in performing.
- Greeks select their own members, which may not always encourage diversity and may hinder your interaction with people outside of the Greek system.
- You may be a target for stereotyping among fellow students who are unfamiliar with the Greek system.

## 2. GREEK VERSUS DORM LIFE

A common requirement of the Greek system is living at your fraternity / sorority Chapter's house for a specific amount of time. However, since many colleges require their students to live on-campus for a specific period of time, living in either a campus dorm or fraternity/sorority Chapter house will usually fulfill this requirement. When deciding whether to live in a campus dorm or fraternity/sorority Chapter house, be sure to consider some of the following differences.

|  | **Greek** | **Dorm** |
| --- | --- | --- |
| **Social Life** | Very Organized & Active | Activity Level Is Your Choice |
| **Living Space** | Entire House | Often Limited To Your Room |
| **Roommates** | Often Your Choice | Roommates Are Assigned |
| **Privacy** | Limited | Some Degree |
| **Cleaning** | You May Be Assigned Responsibility | Less Area To Clean |
| **Food** | You May Be Assigned Responsibility | Provided Through Meal Plans |
| **Social Functions** | Often Mandatory | Activity Level Is Your Choice |
| **Fees** | Vary | Predetermined Amount |

## 3. HOW TO GET INVOLVED IN THE GREEK SYSTEM

Getting involved in the Greek system most often involves "Rushing." This is a process where potential members learn about different fraternities and sororities on campus and then are invited by interested fraternities and sororities to participate in interviews to become a member. Participating in "Rush" does not require you to join, it is simply a time for interested individuals to learn about what the Greek system has to offer. If you decide to "Rush," be sure to consider the following advice.

**Tips For "Rushing"**

- Be yourself, have fun and do not try to be someone you are not.

- When choosing a fraternity or sorority, choose the group that accepts you for who you are, meets your needs, and makes you feel comfortable.
- Conduct research to learn as much as possible about the fraternities or sororities that interest you.  Your knowledge and interest will be extremely valuable during your interviews and will help you choose the fraternity or sorority that is best for you.
- Be sure to consider all of your options by visiting with more than one fraternity or sorority.
- Avoid stereotyping.  What you may hear from others may not actually be correct and you could miss out on a great opportunity.
- Ask as many questions as possible.

**Questions To Ask During "Rush"**
- How much time does it take to pledge?
- Why did you join this fraternity or sorority?
- Is the chapter on probation? If so, why?
- Is the fraternity / sorority national?
- What is the fraternity's / sorority's average Grade Point Average (GPA)?
- What is the GPA requirement for initiation?
- What is the GPA requirement for good standing within the fraternity/sorority?
- Does the fraternity/sorority offer scholarships?
- How much are the monthly/semester dues?
- What is the cost of the affiliation and/or initiation fee?
- What social events are offered during the year?
- Are required social activity fees, such as formals, included in the monthly/semester dues?
- Which type(s) of community service does your chapter perform?
- How active is the fraternity/sorority in campus activities?

## 4. GREEK GLOSSARY

**Active:** an initiated member of a fraternity or sorority.

**Bid:** a formal invitation to pledge for a fraternity or sorority

**Big Brother or Sister:** an active fraternity or a sorority member that serves as a sponsor, advisor, and friend to a new member, and will guide them through their new member programs and the initiation process.

**Chapter:** the local group of the larger national fraternity or sorority.

**Depledge:** the process of dropping out of a fraternity or sorority after joining, but prior to initiation.

**Hazing:** any physical or mental act that puts a person in a stressful or dangerous situation. Almost all colleges have a no-hazing policy and take strict action against any fraternity or sorority that participates in hazing activities.

**Initiation:** the formal ceremony in which new members become active members.

**Legacy:** an individual that has an immediate relative (parent, sibling, or grandparent) who is a member of the fraternity or sorority. Each chapter has its own policy regarding who can be considered a legacy. However, being a legacy does not guarantee an automatic membership into the chapter.

**New Member (Pledge):** an individual that has accepted a bid from a fraternity or sorority.

**Pin:** a fraternity or sorority member's symbol of membership.

**Pledging:** a time period when pledges become more familiar with the chapter.

**Rush:** the period of formal recruitment to meet potential members.

# YOUR HEALTH &
# WELL-BEING

## CHAPTERS

# CAMPUS SAFETY

In most cases, college campuses are safe environments. However, if the opportunity presents itself, some individuals will commit crimes. Therefore, precautions should always be taken to reduce the chance of becoming a victim of a crime. Understand that crimes usually occur when individuals have the chance to commit crimes. Although this section does outline many of these precautions, you are strongly encouraged to visit with the campus police at your college and ask for their advice as to areas/activities you intend to use/participate in. Remember that you are primarily responsible for your own safety and security. The following are safety tips that you may want to consider.

## 1. FUNDAMENTAL CAMPUS SAFETY TIPS

- Take a self-defense course. Most colleges and/or campus police departments offer these courses on a regular basis.
- Report suspicious behavior to campus security.
- Know the current crime trends on your campus by watching local/campus news programs and reading your local/campus newspaper for crime reports.
- Be familiar with your campus surroundings.
- Share your class and activities schedule with your parents and friends, because they should know how to locate you at all times.
- Visit with the campus police department about rules for carrying self-defense items, such as pepper spray.
- Carry a whistle on your key chain and be ready to use it to alert people around you of a crime.
- Purchase a cellular telephone and be sure you know how to use it to reach help immediately.

- Never leave your backpack, purse, or briefcase unattended.
- If at all possible, avoid using Automated Teller Machines at night or in isolated areas.
- Avoid carrying a lot of cash. If you must carry large amounts of cash, place it in an atypical place, such as in your shoe, or use a discrete money pouch that is worn under your clothing.
- Limit the number of valuables you bring with you to college.
- Take important/high-valued items to a safe location when you leave for an extended period of time.
- Decline having your photograph and/or personal information used for public distribution, such as on your college's Web site or directory.
- If you are confronted to give up your valuables, give them up! Your life is far more valuable than losing a few material items or trying to be a hero.

## 2. CAMPUS SAFETY WHILE WALKING

- If at all possible, travel in a group, or at least with a friend.
- Walk on well-lit paths at night.
- Travel on paths that are used by a lot of people.
- If your campus has emergency telephones, be aware of where they are located.
- Utilize escort or shuttle services offered by your campus instead of walking alone to your destination. This process may take a little longer, but is much safer.
- Communicate body language to others that expresses the message that you are calm, confident, and know where you are going.
- Walk between locations as quickly as possible.
- When walking up or down stairwells, through hallways or between buildings, make wide turns or take other measures to be aware of people approaching and/or following you. If you are the least bit concerned for your safety, seek a safe shelter immediately and call for help.

## 3. CAMPUS SAFETY WHILE DRIVING/PARKING YOUR CAR

- Park in well-lit areas as close as possible to your destination.
- When driving, or when parked, secure your car by locking the doors and having all windows completely up.

- When returning to your car, have your keys ready so you can enter the car quickly.
- Prior to entering your car, glance under and inside the car to make sure no one is hiding in or around it.
- If you must keep valuables in your car, store them in the trunk.

## 4. CAMPUS SAFETY FOR OUTDOOR ACTIVITIES

- Avoid jogging and biking at night.
- Choose routes in advance that are safe and well populated.
- Exercise with a friend or group.
- Register your bicycle with the campus police department and purchase sufficient locking mechanisms, such as U-locks and cables.
- Avoid wearing headphones when you walk or bike as they limit your awareness of activities occurring around you.

## 5. PROTECTING YOU & YOUR BELONGINGS ON CAMPUS

- Always keep your doors and windows locked.
- Have emergency telephone numbers easily accessible, such as storing them on your telephone's speed dial system.
- Never lend out your key, access cards, or codes to enter your living area
- Never leave your name on your voicemail.
- Female students should consider having a male friend record their voicemail message for them.
- Never leave messages on your door or voicemail indicating that you will be gone for a period of time.
- Get to know your neighbor(s) and set-up a program to watch out for each other.
- Consider leaving your lights or radio on while you are away from your dorm room or apartment.
- Never leave valuables exposed in your dorm room.
- Consider varying your daily routine so it is not predictable.
- Avoid being alone in isolated places such as laundry rooms, elevators, and stairwells.

# HEALTHY LIVING

The one part of college that students often fail to succeed at is maintaining a healthy lifestyle. Although maintaining a healthy lifestyle during college can be difficult, there are many benefits to maintaining a healthy lifestyle, such as an increase in energy, and the ability to work, think and concentrate more efficiently. This section will provide you with tips on maintaining a healthy lifestyle in college by addressing the major components of a healthy lifestyle, including diet, exercise, sleep, and stress. Please be aware that the following information is only provided as a guide and is not a substitute for professional medical advice or treatment. If you are concerned about the health of your lifestyle, consult your college physician or healthcare professional.

## 1. DIET

You may be aware of the term "Freshman 15." This term refers to the average amount of weight (15 pounds) a student will gain during their first year of college. Often maintaining a regular balanced diet is extremely hard for college students, particularly freshmen, because, for the first time in their lives, they are in charge of making the decision on what they eat. Because of this, many students develop poor eating habits and soon notice an increase in their body weight.

There are a number of reference materials available to help you establish a regular balanced diet. Your college physician or healthcare professional can assist you in locating these materials and/or developing a regular balanced diet that meets your specific needs. On the next page are some general tips that may assist you in keeping off that "Freshman 15."

**Common Causes Of The "Freshman 15"**
- Unfamiliarity in developing a regular balanced diet
- Eating whenever, and whatever, you want
- Eating at irregular intervals or late at night
- Consuming large amounts of foods and drinks that are high in fat and calories, such as fast food, pizza or alcoholic beverages
- Eating to cope with stress (see the "Stress" portion of this section) or other feelings
- Lack of sleep (see the "Sleep" portion of this section)
- Limited, or no regular exercise (see the "Exercise" portion of this section)

**How To Prevent The "Freshman 15"**
The most effective method of preventing the "Freshman 15," or other unhealthy lifestyle habit, is to consult your college physician or healthcare professional. In addition, most colleges are now offering introductory "Healthy Living" education courses that students can take as an elective course. Use the information you gather from these resources, as well as the tips provided in this section, to develop a program for maintaining a healthy lifestyle. You may find it helpful to develop goals as part of your healthy living program. To learn more about developing, and accomplishing, goals, review the "Goals" section on page 28.

## 2. EXERCISE
Being active and maintaining a regular exercise program is important for many reasons, such as overall physical and mental strength. Even though exercising offers many great benefits, most people view maintaining a regular exercise program as a chore they **must** do. This should not be the situation at all. In fact, developing a "fun" exercise program can be particularly easy for college students, since there are so many activities from which to choose and participate. Listed below are just a few suggestions on how to implement more exercise into your daily schedule. Please remember that the following information is only provided as a guide and is not a substitute for professional medical advice or treatment. If you are concerned about starting an exercise program, you should consult your college physician or healthcare professional.

- Develop an exercise program that you can follow and be sure to develop goals that you want to accomplish. There are a number of great resources on developing exercise programs available through your college library or bookstore. In addition, your college physician, healthcare professional, or fitness trainer can assist you in developing an exercise program that is best for you. Without some type of program to follow, you can lose focus on what you are trying to accomplish and may find it difficult to exercise regularly. Be sure to read the "Goals" section on page 28 for more information about developing and establishing goals.

- Enroll in a physical education course. Most colleges offer physical education courses as elective courses. These courses are a great way to implement exercise into your schedule and to meet new people.

- Create a progress report of your exercise program and place it in a location that you will see frequently. Progress reports are great motivators and can also provide positive reinforcement. You can chart your progress by using a notebook, a poster board, a calendar, or even your computer.

- Take advantage of your college's exercise facilities. In most cases, access to these facilities is free to students.

- Inquire about non-course related exercise classes, such as aerobics or spinning, which may be offered at your college exercise facility. These are usually offered for free to students.

- Consider walking or biking to your classes versus taking the bus or driving. This simple task can make a big difference after one semester or quarter.

- If your college's gym hours do not coordinate with your schedule, consider joining a community gym with longer hours. In many cases, they will offer student discounts. Another alternative is to invest in a small weight set for use in your apartment or dorm, such as a set of dumbbells.

- Find an exercise partner. Having someone else dependent on you for working out is a great motivator. Therefore, invite classmates or friends that share your interest in maintaining a healthy lifestyle to exercise with you.

- Make exercise a social activity. Most colleges offer students the ability to participate in a variety of intramural sporting activities, such as bowling, softball, basketball or flag football. In addition, check with your student activities office and ask about programs they offer. Common programs include skiing, whitewater rafting, and hiking/biking trips. Although these trips may not be free, they are usually offered at significant discounts. They are also a great way to meet new people.

## 3. SLEEP

Sleep is just as important, if not more so, as a healthy diet and exercise. Not getting enough sleep can cause your body to become weak and cause your brain to work less effectively. The normal amount of sleep that a college-aged student (ages 18-24) requires is at least seven to eight hours. This section will provide you with tips on how to get enough sleep, as well as tips on how to make your sleep time comfortable. However, if the tips provided below do not assist you in obtaining a sufficient amount of sleep, you should consult your college physician or healthcare professional for assistance.

### Achieving The Proper Amount Of Sleep

- Develop a regular sleep schedule. Fluctuating your sleep time can cause problems in obtaining the proper amount of sleep needed. You may find it helpful to review the "Time Management" section on page 82 to develop a proper sleep schedule.
- Take a nap during the day if needed. When your body requires more sleep, it will let you know. Feeling tired during the day, or having trouble staying awake during a class, are signs that your body is not getting enough sleep. By listening to your body and taking a nap, you will feel much better and more active.
- Avoid "all-nighters." Staying up most of the night, or all night, in order to prepare for an exam is not an effective study method. In most cases, depriving your body of sleep will cause you more problems on your exam than trying to feed your tired mind more information than it is capable of recalling the next day.
- Relax before you go to sleep. Relaxing allows your body and mind to release tension and will allow you to fall asleep more easily. Some methods of relaxation include reading an enjoyable book, listening to music, watching television, or surfing the Internet.

- Maintain a proper diet and exercise program. More information regarding these topics is located earlier in this section.
- Avoid taking a bath or shower prior to going to sleep, as they tend to stimulate your body.
- Avoid consuming beverages with caffeine or alcohol before going to sleep. Caffeine and alcohol can act as a stimulant and cause frequent awakenings and shallow sleep.
- If you smoke, avoid smoking before going to bed as nicotine acts as a stimulant causing difficulty for your body to fall, and stay, asleep.
- Avoid the use of medication to assist you in sleeping. Frequent use of this medication can cause dependency or serious sleep problems.
- Create a relaxing atmosphere in your bedroom. For example, make sure that your room is not excessively warm or cold and minimize noise and light.

## 4. STRESS

Stress is a mental, physical, and emotional strain that can be caused by any number of situations. Stress is a natural reaction and, when controlled, can be beneficial. For example, the reaction of stress can cause your body to become energized and motivated to correct the situation that is causing the stress to occur, such as completing a difficult assignment or developing a study program for an upcoming exam. However, stress, when not controlled, can be dangerous. So dangerous that it can cause mental burnout and/or physical exhaustion. Provided below is a list of some of the symptoms of stress, as well as tips on how to control stress in your life. If you believe you are suffering from excessive stress, please consult your college physician or healthcare professional for assistance.

**Symptoms Of Stress**
The following conditions could be symptoms of excessive stress.
- **Physical**
  Dramatic weight loss/gain, frequent headaches, constant fatigue, diarrhea, sleeplessness or excessive sleep, muscular tightness or spasms
- **Emotional**
  Easily angered or frustrated, nervousness, irritability, dramatic mood swings

- **Mental**
Frequently confused, lack of interest in previously entertaining activities, loss of concentration, forgetfulness

**Coping With Stress**
Although the most desirable situation would be to rid yourself of the situation that is causing you stress, this is not always an available option. If you are not able to rid yourself of the situation that is causing you stress, then consider utilizing some of the tips listed below as methods to cope with your stress.

- Get organized and avoid procrastinating. Not being able to manage your time effectively is a major cause of stress. Review the "Time Management" section on page 82 for more information.
- Keep negative situations in perspective. For example, receiving a bad grade or having a fight with your significant other can be difficult, but they are not the end of your world. Focus on overcoming these obstacles and achieving greater opportunities.
- Avoid dwelling on large tasks that need to be completed. Instead, develop a plan to complete smaller tasks that will eventually allow you to complete the large task.
- Maintain a healthy lifestyle. The better you feel physically, the better you will feel mentally. In addition, exercising is a great release of tension and stress.
- Avoid working on difficult problems for long periods of time. Take frequent breaks and do something you enjoy.
- Focus on the positive aspects of a situation. For example, if you find out that your Chemistry 101 exam is now one week earlier than originally planned, you could stress out about how much information you need to study by that time, or you could focus on the positive aspect of taking the exam earlier, which is that you will be able to start your Christmas break one week earlier.
- Schedule fun, relaxing activities into your weekly schedule.
- Visit with friends or family about your stressful situation. Many times, just talking to someone about what you are dealing with will help put the situation into perspective and relieve some, or all, of the stress associated with it.

# HOMESICKNESS

Being homesick is a normal feeling many new students experience, particularly during their first term at college. This feeling, which usually disappears within a few weeks, occurs as a result of being placed into a new environment with new people and at the same time feeling vulnerable, lonely and insecure. Homesickness does take some effort to overcome, but remember, the more effort you put into overcoming homesickness, the quicker you will overcome it. Listed below are a few tips to help you overcome homesickness as quickly as possible.

### Overcoming Homesickness

- Remember that you are not alone. There are often hundreds, even thousands, of other students around you that are experiencing the same feelings that you are. Help yourself, and others, overcome these feelings by introducing yourself and opening the lines of communication. Often, opening the lines of communication is as easy as just saying "Hi."

- Take the lead. Ask other new students you interact with to participate in activities together with you, such as attending a movie, going to lunch together, ordering a pizza for dinner, or even coming over to your room to hang out one evening.

- Go on an adventure and familiarize yourself with your surroundings. Even better, ask another new student to go with you. Get a map of campus and go see the different areas on campus. The more familiar you become with campus, the less strange it will feel to you.

- Avoid secluding yourself in your room or apartment. Go to public areas, participate in campus activities, and get involved. Refer to the "Campus Activities" section on page 89 for more information.

- Bring articles from home to decorate your room/apartment at school to give it a familiar feel. The more comfortable you feel in your room/apartment, the more relaxed you will become.
- Control the amount of time you spend visiting with your family or friends via telephone, email or return trips home. Although contacting family and friends can be comforting, too much contact can cause your homesickness to become worse.
- If you are having difficulty overcoming your homesickness, visit with someone about your feelings. There are a number of people on campus available to assist you, such as your resident advisor, academic advisor, school counselor, or religious counselor.

# UNDERSTANDING YOUR FINANCES

## CHAPTERS

# BANKING

Banking is a fact of life. However, does it make sense to pay someone, in the form of various fees, to use your own money? Of course not, but it is how many financial institutions do business. By finding the right financial institution to match your needs, you can save a significant amount of money. This section will provide you with the tools to assist you in evaluating the best financial institution to meet your needs. In addition, this section will address some basic tips on how to balance your financial accounts.

## 1. BANKS & CREDIT UNIONS - THE DIFFERENCES

### Banks
Banks are financial institutions that receive, lend, and safeguard money. Many banks also offer a variety of services, such as financial planning and safe-deposit box rentals. Banks can be divided into either local or national banks.

### Local Banks
Local banks service a small community or region. They are generally owned and operated by members of the community in which they are located. Due to the nature of local banks, they generally offer services that specifically cater to the community where they are located. Local banks also tend to understand the needs of the customer. For instance, if a long-time customer of a local bank needed a short-term loan in order to purchase an airline ticket to see a sick relative, a local bank is likely to work with that person because of their relationship with the bank.

**National Banks**
National banks are financial institutions that are generally owned by
investors. National banks offer many of the same services as local banks;
however, because of their size, national banks can offer more services and
usually at a better rate. Due to their larger size, national banks have
difficulty catering their services to local communities and often lack the
ability to take personal circumstances into consideration when determining
eligibility for financial services. Therefore, national banks will frequently
develop a one-size-fits-all product, such as a "College Student
Savings/Checking Program."

**Credit Unions**
Similar to banks, credit unions are financial institutions that receive, lend,
and safeguard money. Credit unions also offer their customers a variety of
financial services. The primary difference between a bank and credit union
is that a credit union is managed and operated by a non-profit cooperative
group. For example, state and government employees often have credit
unions that they can participate in. Since credit unions are non-profit, they
can offer very competitive interest rates on accounts and loans, and they
frequently do not charge for many of the same services that banks charge
for, such as using a non-associated Automated Teller Machine (ATM).

Because federal law regulates credit union membership, you need to be part
of a particular group to be eligible for membership. To determine if you are
eligible to join a credit union, consider the following:
1. Contact local credit unions and ask them their requirements for
   membership.
2. Contact your employer to determine if they are associated with a
   credit union.
3. Ask your family members if they belong to a credit union. Many
   credit unions offer membership to immediate family members.
4. Some credit unions base membership eligibility on geographic
   location. Therefore, ask your neighbors about local credit unions
   you may be eligible for.

## 2. DETERMINING YOUR NEEDS
Understanding your financial institution needs is very important for two
reasons. First, it is important to know what services to look for when
opening an account with a financial institution. Second, it makes you aware

of what fees you are currently paying and how to avoid paying those fees in the future.

To understand your financial institution needs, collect your bank statements for the past six months and complete the chart provided below.

| Month | 1 | 2 | 3 | 4 | 5 | 6 | Average |
|---|---|---|---|---|---|---|---|
| Number Of Checks Written | | | | | | | |
| Number Of ATM Withdrawals | | | | | | | |
| Fees: | | | | | | | |
|     ATM Usage | | | | | | | |
|     Account Maintenance | | | | | | | |
|     Overdraft | | | | | | | |
|     Others: (Describe Each) | | | | | | | |
|     1) | | | | | | | |
|     2) | | | | | | | |
|     3) | | | | | | | |
| Interest Rate On Savings Acct. | | | | | | | |
| Interest Rate On Checking Acct. | | | | | | | |

Once you have completed this chart, evaluate your usage pattern. Visit with your current financial institution, as well as others in your area, to determine if there are methods that you can implement in order to reduce various fees or charges you frequently incur.

If you have not previously had a checking or savings account, visit with financial institutions in your area and ask them to describe the different financial programs they have to offer. Locate the program that offers the most flexibility. Thus, as your needs change, so does your financial program. In addition, try to locate a program that offers the most benefits and has the least amount of fees associated with the program.

## 3. INTERNET USE
Many financial institutions offer account access through the Internet. To encourage customers to use this service and avoid using tellers, financial institutions provide incentives such as waiving normal fees for transfers or account inquiries. This service is very convenient and efficient for

customers who cannot travel to the financial institution's location for ordinary banking needs and that do not have the time to stand in line.

## 4. AUTOMATED TELLER MACHINES (ATMs)

When using an ATM, be aware of your financial institution's ATM usage fee, as some financial institutions will not charge a fee for using ATMs that they own. Other institutions (commonly credit unions) will allow you to use ATMs at locations other than their own without incurring a fee. However, these financial institutions usually limit the usage of these types of programs. For example, the first 10 ATM uses per month may be free, and then each additional use is at a fee of $1 per transaction.

## 5. DEBIT & CHECK CARDS

There are several advantages and disadvantages associated with using debit cards. One advantage is that debit cards are easy to qualify for. As long as you do not have a bad credit history, you will most likely qualify for a debit card. Other advantages are that debit cards are more readily accepted than checks, identification is not required when using a debit card, and there is no need to carry cash or a checkbook.

One disadvantage of a debit card as compared to a checkbook or credit card is that funds are automatically taken out of your account. When using a checkbook or credit card, you are provided a slight delay in the transfer of funds or in the payment of the expense. Other disadvantages of a debit card are that it is difficult to record transactions, debit cards are likely to have fees associated with their use, and debit card statements do not normally offer a detailed list of purchases as credit card statements do.

## 6. OBTAINING PRINTED CHECKS

Inquire about free printed checks from your financial institution as many institutions offer this service when you open a new account. If you need to purchase your printed checks, avoid purchasing them from your financial institution because the average charge is between $12 and $17 for a box of 250 checks. Instead, order printed checks from either a company on the Internet or from advertisers in the Sunday newspaper, as these tend to be less expensive than what a financial institution would charge. Furthermore, consider changing companies with each order you make. By doing so, you will receive "first-time ordering" discounts.

## 7. BALANCING YOUR ACCOUNTS

Balancing your accounts on a regular basis is essential to avoiding costly mistakes and establishing a poor credit history. These steps will assist you in balancing your accounts correctly.

### Record Your Use/Addition Of Funds

Keeping track of where you are using your funds is not only important for banking purposes, but also establishing a budget (see the "Budgeting" section on page 115). Below are some tips on how to track your use of funds.

- If you use a debit card, keep a register to track your usage.
- Purchase duplicate checks so that you have a copy available for reference.
- Write ATM withdrawls/deposits into your account register immediately. You may find it helpful to keep your ATM receipt in your wallet as an additional reference.
- When depositing funds, note the date the funds were deposited and when they will be available. Also keep a copy of the deposit slip for reference.
- Establish a set time each week, such as Sunday evening, to review your financial accounts and update any activity that may have been forgotten.

### Balancing Your Accounts

Each month, your financial institution will provide you with a statement outlining the activities that have occurred to your accounts during that period of time. When you receive this statement, you should compare the information to your own information in your account registers. You may also find it helpful to check this information on a more frequent interval. This can be accomplished with Internet access to your accounts or by requesting a current statement from your financial institution (*be aware, there may be a charge for this service*). The tips below will assist you in balancing your accounts.

- Compare your monthly bank statement against your account registers, and place a check next to, or highlight, each transaction in your register that is recorded on your bank statement.
- Add to your account registers any deposits or additions including interest payments and ATM or electronic deposits listed on the statement that are not already entered.

- Subtract from your account register any account deductions including fees and ATM or electronic deductions that are not already entered.
- Compare any withdrawl/deposit slips and the amounts of any checks you have written with your bank statement for errors in amounts. Having these slips, or duplicate checks, may be your only method of proving an error has occurred, so it is important to keep these.
- Most financial institution statements have a balance sheet located on the backside of the statement. If not, contact your financial institution for a balance sheet form. Follow the directions to complete the balance sheet and determine your current ending balance. Match the results with the balance in your account register. If the two balances match, you have balanced your account correctly. However, if the two balances do not match, check your calculations. If you are unable to resolve the difference, contact your financial institution for assistance.

# BUDGETING

Budgeting involves understanding where your money comes from and where your money is spent, saved, or invested. Most students' think that budgeting is something you should do after you finish college and get job, but this is not true. Creating and maintaining a budget while you are at college will not only help you develop a strong understanding of your financial boundaries, but it can also help you start your life after college with the least amount of debt possible.

## 1. IDENTIFY YOUR FINANCIAL GOALS

If you are like most college students, you may view your financial goals as trying to get enough money to pay for tuition and books and then hopefully have enough money left over to buy some food and pay your rent. But in most instances, this is not really the case.

Start a list of your top ten to fifteen financial goals. Create a list of short- (the current school term, such as a quarter or semester) and long-term (6 months or more) financial goals. Goals can be anything that is important to you, such as buying a new outfit or compact disc, paying off all your bills each month, buying an airline ticket home for the holidays, saving money for a spring-break trip, or even just saving a few dollars a month in case of an emergency. By establishing your financial goals, you create an incentive to stay focused on developing and maintaining your personal budget. Two charts for listing your short- and long-term goals have been provided on the next page.

## 2. RANK YOUR GOALS

Once you have established your short- and long-term financial goals, rank them according to their importance to you. This will be used as your progress chart.   Make a copy of your goals and place them somewhere where you will see them frequently as a reminder.

### Short-Term Goals

| Goal | Expense | Time-Frame | Rank |
|------|---------|------------|------|
| Ex. New Clothes | $25 | Monthly | |
| | | | |
| | | | |
| | | | |
| | | | |
| | | | |
| | | | |
| | | | |
| | | | |
| | | | |
| | | | |
| | | | |

### Long-Term Goals

| Goal | Expense | Time-Frame | Rank |
|------|---------|------------|------|
| Ex. Spring-break trip | $500 | April 10, 2006 | |
| | | | |
| | | | |
| | | | |
| | | | |
| | | | |
| | | | |
| | | | |
| | | | |
| | | | |
| | | | |
| | | | |

## 3. DETERMINE YOUR INCOME

Determining your income can be difficult for college students since you may not have a steady monthly income.  However, income can be generated from a variety of resources, such as financial aid, scholarships, contributions from your parents, or pay from a part-time job.  A chart has been provided below to calculate your income.  **Use income you receive after taxes.**

### Income

| Source | Amount | Occurrence |
|--------|--------|------------|
| Ex. Financial Aid | $3,356 | Each Semester |
| Ex. Pay From Work | $250 | Twice a month |
| Ex. Parent Contribution | $100 | Monthly |
| | | |
| | | |
| | | |
| | | |
| Total: | | |
| Average/Month: | | |

## 4. DETERMINE YOUR FIXED EXPENSES

Every month, as well as yearly, there are a number of fixed expenses you need to pay. Having an understanding of when these expenses occur will assist you in developing a budget that plans for these expenses.

When filling out the Monthly Fixed Expense chart below and the Yearly Fixed Expense chart on the next page, place all your known expenses where they occur and estimate where the others tend to occur. For example, on the Monthly Fixed Expense chart, place the cable bill on the day of the month it occurs. On the Yearly Fixed Expense chart, only list those expenses that do not occur each month, such as holiday gifts, automobile license fees, and magazine subscriptions. You will notice that the Yearly Expense Chart has a monthly average section, which means to take the total expenses and divide by twelve. This amount will be deducted from your income along with your monthly fixed expenses. However, this amount will be placed in a safe account, such as a savings account. As these various fixed expenses occur throughout the year, you will have sufficient funding available to pay for them.

### Monthly Fixed Expenses
Examples include Rent, Cable & Auto Insurance

| 1 Ex: Rent $500 | 12 | 23 |
|---|---|---|
| 2 | 13 | 24 |
| 3 | 14 | 25 |
| 4 | 15 | 26 |
| 5 | 16 | 27 |
| 6 | 17 | 28 |
| 7 | 18 | 29 |
| 8 | 19 | 30 |
| 9 | 20 | 31 |
| 10 | 21 | |
| 11 | 22 | Monthly Total: |

## Yearly Fixed Expenses

Examples include Gifts (Holiday/Birthday), Automobile Registration, and Subscriptions

| | |
|---|---|
| **January** | Ex: Automobile Registration - $125 |
| **February** | |
| **March** | |
| **April** | |
| **May** | |
| **June** | |
| **July** | |
| **August** | |
| **September** | |
| **October** | |
| **November** | |
| **December** | |
| **Total** | |
| **Monthly Average (Total/12)** | |

## 5. DETERMINE YOUR VARIABLE EXPENSES

Determining your variable expenses can be difficult. Variable expenses include everything that is not included in "Fixed Expenses" and vary in their occurrence or expense each month. For example, groceries, snacks, entertainment, gasoline, long-distance telephone charges, and clothing purchases would all be included in this section. To keep track of your variable expenses try some of these suggestions:

- Keep a small notepad/piece of paper and pen with you at all times to record where you spend your money.
- Request receipts for all of your purchases. Purchase duplicate checks or write a detailed description of your purchases in your check register.

- Spend a few minutes every evening to record your daily variable expenses.
- Spend an hour each week to review your daily variable expenses and calculate totals.

When filling out these charts you will notice a section for credit cards. All purchases made on credit are to be listed under the particular section where the purchase belongs. For example, if you purchase $10 of gasoline for your car on credit card, you would list $10 in the automobile section. The credit card section is to be used for those people who have prior credit card balances and may not recall what the expenses were used for. Place payments made toward that previous balance in this section of the chart. A separate section is located just below the credit card section to place any fees (interest, late, etc.) you may have incurred.

Provided below is a daily variable expense chart (for one week) and on the next page is a weekly variable expense chart (for four weeks). Make copies of these charts as needed.

## Daily Variable Expenses

|  | Daily |
|---|---|
| Automobile |  |
| Household |  |
| Snacks |  |
| Entertainment |  |
| Laundry |  |
| Groceries |  |
| Personal Care (Haircut, etc.) |  |
| Utilities |  |
| Credit Card |  |
| Fees (Interest, Late Fees, etc.) |  |
| Other: |  |
|  |  |
|  |  |
|  |  |
|  |  |
|  |  |
|  |  |
| Totals |  |

## Weekly Variable Expenses

| Week | 1 | 2 | 3 | 4 | Totals |
|---|---|---|---|---|---|
| Automobile | | | | | |
| Household | | | | | |
| Snacks | | | | | |
| Entertainment | | | | | |
| Laundry | | | | | |
| Groceries | | | | | |
| Personal Care | | | | | |
| Utilities | | | | | |
| Credit Card | | | | | |
| Fees | | | | | |
| Other: | | | | | |
| | | | | | |
| | | | | | |
| | | | | | |
| | | | | | |
| | | | | | |
| Totals | | | | | |

## 6. PUT IT ALL TOGETHER

Once you have completed all the charts (a total of one month of budgeting), place the information you have gathered into the chart provided below.

## Totals

| | |
|---|---|
| Total Monthly Income (TMI) | |
| | |
| Monthly Fixed Expenses | |
| Yearly Fixed Expenses (Monthly Payment) | |
| Monthly Variable Expenses | |
| Total Monthly Expenses (TME) | |
| TMI – TME | |

## 7. EVALUATING THE RESULTS

The results of filling out the chart above will provide one of two outcomes regarding your financial status you are either living within your means or you are not. The results also tell you if you are capable of meeting the financial goals you established for yourself earlier in this section.

### You Are Living Above Your Means

If the total from the "Totals" chart on page 120 was a negative number, you are living above your means. Beware, this is a very serious situation and should be addressed as soon as possible. The first thing to do if you are living above your means is to evaluate your budget. If there are areas in your budget where you can reduce your expenses, do so. In most cases, reducing your expenses is far easier than increasing your income. If you review your budget and there are no areas of the budget that can be reduced, then you may need to seek professional assistance.

### You Are Living Within Your Means

If the total from the "Totals" chart on page 120 was a positive number, you are living within your means. This is a great accomplishment and you should be very proud of yourself. Not everyone is capable of accomplishing this goal. However, just because you are living within your means does not necessarily mean you are meeting your financial goals. To determine if you are meeting your financial goals, complete the chart on page 122.

*Example:*
*Assume there is $70 remaining after all expenses have been paid. Earlier in this section, a short-term goal of $25 per month to purchase clothes was given. Another goal was to acquire $500 for a spring break trip in April 2006. This example budget is starting January 2005. Therefore, this person has 15 months of about $34 each month to acquire the $500 needed for the trip.*

| Remaining Funds (After Fixed/Variable Expenses) | Ex: $70 |
| --- | --- |
| Goals: | |
| Ex: Clothes | Ex: -$25 |
| Ex: Car Down Payment | Ex: -$34 |
| Total Remaining (After Goals) | Ex: $11 |

In the example, this person is living within their means and is meeting their goals. On top of that, they also have remaining funds. Under this situation, this person should consider investing the remaining amount in a savings account or other fund.

## 8. HOW OFTEN SHOULD YOU BUDGET?

When establishing a budget, you should complete all the sections/charts above for at least three consecutive months. Once you have completed those three months, you have done all the hard work. However, this does not mean you are done. Budgeting should become a normal part of your life. As you accept more responsibility in your life or major changes occur, the more important budgeting your finances will become. For example, if you decide you want to attend graduate school or purchase a car, being capable of understanding your financial situation will be imperative. Therefore, at least once a year, as well as any time there is a major change in your lifestyle or financial goals (for example when you accept a new part-time job or receive a raise in your pay), you should update your budget.

## 9. ADDITIONAL BUDGET RESOURCES

There are numerous resources available to assist you in developing and maintaining a budget, including books, software, and professionals. Regardless if you are having difficulty establishing a budget or you are an avid budgeter, you should seek out these additional resources. The more information you have about budgeting and the better you understand your financial goals, the more efficient you will be in accomplishing your financial goals. These resources can be found in your local library, a bookstore, the Internet, and many financial institutions.

# CREDIT CARDS

College students are prime targets for credit card companies. This will become very apparent as you begin to receive solicitations for credit cards in the mail on a regular basis and begin to be bombarded by credit card company booths at college events offering free T-shirts or other items just for applying for a credit card. The reason companies do this is that they hope that by locking you into a credit card early in life, you will keep their credit card after you graduate and become a prime credit card consumer.

However, with credit card debt continually rising among college students, credit cards have proven to be a financially dangerous tool among college students. Yet, if used properly, having a credit card can be a valuable tool in establishing a good credit history. This section will provide insight into the use of credit cards, such as the benefits of having a credit card, what credit card you should use, and how to avoid getting into credit card debt. In addition, this section will provide you with some suggestions on negotiating better terms with your credit card company.

## 1. TYPES OF CREDIT CARDS
There are primarily two different types of credit cards: a credit card and a charge card. A description of each follows.

### Credit Card
Credit cards entitle the user to a revolving line-of-credit with no interest fees on purchases, if the outstanding balance of that line-of-credit is paid in full by each due date. However, if the outstanding balance of that line-of-credit is not paid in full, interest fees will apply to the remaining balance as well as applied immediately to all future purchases. In addition, interest fees are charged immediately to all cash advances at the time the cash advance is made. The value of the line-of-credit, interest rate and applicable charges

are determined by a number of factors, including the borrower's credit risk and annual income.

## Charge Card

A charge card is very similar to a credit card; however, with a charge card the user must make full payment on the outstanding balance each month. For use of the line-of-credit, an annual fee is usually assessed. Large interest rates and late fees will be applied to balances that are not paid in full on the due date. As with a credit card, the value of the line-of-credit is determined by a number of factors, including the borrower's credit risk and annual income.

## 2. BENEFITS OF A CREDIT CARD

Credit cards provide their users various benefits. Listed below are the primary benefits credit cards can provide.

## Security

Credit cards provide the user a method of payment when cash is unavailable and personal checks can not be used. For example, when travelling you may have an occasion to use them, such as when your car breaks down, where you have insufficient cash and personal checks are not accepted. In this situation, having a credit card enables you to make your payment.

## Establishing Credit

Establishing credit, particularly for young adults, is difficult but important. Receiving credit from a major credit card company and properly using it are great ways to establish your credit history. Establishing a good credit history will allow you to receive important loans later in life, for example when applying for a loan to purchase a new car or home.

## Flexibility

Credit cards provide the user flexibility in their budget. When properly used, a credit card may provide the user forty-five (45) days or more of free credit. Consider the example below.

*Example: Your credit card has a billing date of the 5$^{th}$ of every month. Payment for that credit card is to be received by the 15$^{th}$ of every month. Therefore, if you make a purchase on the 6$^{th}$, that purchase will not show up*

*until the following month and will not be due until the 15th of that month.*
*Assuming that you pay off the balance of that purchase on time, you have*
*just been provided use of that credit card company's money for almost 45*
*days with no interest or fees.*

### Insurance
Many credit card companies offer customers insurance coverage on
purchases made with the company's credit card. The details and specifics of
this coverage vary from credit card company to credit card company.
Therefore, contact credit card companies you are considering and ask them
to provide you details and examples of how the insurance coverage works.

### Free Stuff
Credit card companies offer customers a variety of promotions, many of
which include free items, including T-shirts, movie tickets, gasoline, and
even air travel. Before signing up for a card that is offering a promotional
item you want, be sure to pay particular attention to the details of the card,
such as the interest rate, annual fees, and what you need to do in order to
earn the free stuff. In many cases, just purchasing the free item would be
cheaper and easier than struggling with the steps to acquire it from the credit
card company.

## 3. AVOIDING CREDIT CARD DEBT
Credit cards offer a number of benefits for stringent users. However,
because of the easy access to credit and lack of budgeting skills, some credit
card users find themselves charging their credit cards far above their means.
Below are suggestions to implement in order to stay out of credit card debt.

### Keep One Card
Most people have a need for only one credit card. Therefore, find a credit
card that offers a number of advantages and then cancel any other cards you
have.

### Use A Charge Card
To keep from going into credit card debt, apply for a charge card. Charge
cards require the entire outstanding balance to be paid in full each month.

### Establish A Credit Limit

If you have a problem purchasing too many items on your credit card each month, but just are unwilling to get rid of your card, contact your credit card company and request your available credit be reduced to an amount you are able to pay off every month.

### Consolidate Outstanding Balances

If you have several credit cards with outstanding balances, find the credit card with the lowest interest rate and consolidate your other credit card balances to that card. This will enable you to see your complete debt on one statement and the progress you make in paying the balance off.

### Reduce The Interest Rate

If you have an outstanding credit card balance, or are considering consolidating other outstanding credit card balances to just one credit card, contact the credit card company you are considering consolidating the cards to and negotiate for a better interest rate. When negotiating, simply state you want to consolidate your other outstanding credit card balances and wish to consolidate them with their company. Ask to have a special interest rate applied to the consolidated amount. If they hesitate in offering you a special interest rate, suggest that you will use another company.

### Keep A Journal

One of the problems with credit cards is that customers are unaware of their credit card balance until the statement arrives each month. By keeping a journal of your credit card purchases throughout the month, you will be aware of the exact outstanding balance on your card.

### Stop Using Credit

In order to pay off your debts, you need to stop using your credit card. The most effective method to stop using your card to purchase items is to cut up your credit card until the debt is paid. If you encounter an emergency where you need to use the card, you can contact the credit card company by telephone to have a purchase credited to your account.

### Budget Monthly Payments

To assist in paying off your credit card debt, create a budget. (Read the "Budgeting" section on page 115 to determine how to make a budget work for you.)  Designate a specific amount in your budget to be used toward paying off the outstanding balance of your credit card each month.

### Avoid Late Fees / Bad Credit

Late fees can be obtained two ways: not making your monthly payment on time or paying less than the minimum amount.  In addition to being expensive, late fees are also a sign of bad credit and will show up on your credit report.  To avoid these fees, contact your credit card company. Inform them of your financial situation and request assistance.  Common assistance will include changing your billing period so that your payment due date will occur at a more convenient time or lowering your monthly minimum.  Lowering your monthly payment will cause your balance to be paid off over a longer amount of time and increase the amount of interest you will have to pay, but it will keep your credit history clean until you are able to make additional contributions toward the balance.

## 4. ANNUAL FEES & INTEREST RATES

Annual fees and interest rates are the primary tools credit card companies use to make money.  Before you accept a credit card, be sure you understand these two components of the credit card.

### Annual Fees

Some credit cards charge an annual fee.  Frequently, these are credit cards that are offering valuable benefits to their customers, such as frequent flier mileage or insurance coverage on purchases.  Unless you use your credit card frequently and charge large amounts to it, paying an annual fee is not necessary.  There are numerous credit cards to choose from that do not charge an annual fee and provide excellent benefits.

### Interest Rates

In many instances, credit cards offering the best promotions, such as cash back or free gifts, also charge the highest interest rates.  Therefore, as long as you can pay off your monthly balance each month, interest rates are not that important.  However, if you must carry a monthly balance, evaluate the interest rates carefully.  In particular, pay special attention to introductory rates.  These introductory offers tend to expire quickly and often result in an extremely high interest rate credit card.

## 5. APPLYING FOR A CREDIT CARD

Before completing a credit card application, be sure to read the application carefully. If you have any questions about information on the application, contact the credit card company and ask them to explain any confusing parts. Be sure to pay particular attention to the small print. For example, many credit cards offer an introductory low interest rate. The small print should explain the terms of this offer and when you can expect the interest rate to rise and to what level the interest rate will rise. Finally, make a copy of your application and store it in a safe location in case you need to refer to the contract agreement at a later date.

## 6. PROTECTING YOURSELF FROM CREDIT CARD FRAUD

Credit card fraud is a terrible situation to experience and can be extremely costly if you do not protect yourself. Many credit card companies offer some type of fraud protection, such as limiting the financial amount you will be responsible for. Be sure to contact your credit card company and be aware of their fraud protection policy. If you do not believe the policy is sufficient, consider switching to a credit card company that offers a policy that meets your needs. Listed below are tips on how to protect yourself from credit card fraud:

- Always keep your credit card statements and receipts in a safe location.
- Never give your credit card number over the phone to strangers or use it on Internet sites that you are unfamiliar with.
- Never write down your Personal Identification Number (PIN). Create one that you can memorize easily.
- When throwing away documents with your credit card number on them, be sure to tear them up sufficiently.
- Keep the telephone number of your credit card company in a location other than your wallet so that if your wallet/credit card is stolen, you can contact the credit card company immediately.
- Keep your credit cards in a safe location.

# CREDIT REPORT

Your credit report is used by a number of organizations, such as potential creditors, employers, and landlords. The information is provided as a service to these organizations so that they are aware of the financial risk (possible default) you present to them. Therefore, understanding and ensuring that the information in your credit report is accurate and complete is very important. Provided in this section is a list of your rights under the Fair Credit Reporting Act (FCRA), information on how to request a credit report, as well as details on how to obtain a copy of your credit report for free.

## 1. YOUR RIGHTS

The FCRA was established to provide accuracy, fairness, and privacy of information in the files of consumer reporting agencies. These agencies are credit bureaus that gather and sell information about you, such as if you pay your bills on time, if you have filed for bankruptcy, and how much credit you are eligible for. In addition, the FCRA provides the individual specific rights regarding the information contained within credit reports. These rights include the following:

### Who Uses Information Against You?

Anyone who uses information gathered from a credit report to take action against you, such as denying you credit or employment, must provide you with the name, address, and telephone number of the credit reporting agency that provided them the information they used as the basis for their action.

## Disputing Inaccurate Information

If you believe information listed in your credit report is inaccurate, you can dispute the information. First, contact the credit reporting agency about your dispute. The credit reporting agency must investigate the items within 30 days by presenting to its information source all relevant evidence you submit, unless your dispute is frivolous. The source must review your evidence and report its findings to the credit reporting agency. If the source was in error, the source must also advise other national credit reporting agencies to which it has provided data of any error. The credit reporting agency must then provide you a written report of the investigation and a report if the investigation results in a change.

If the investigation does not resolve the dispute, you can add a brief statement to your file for organizations requesting to see your information. In addition, if the information in dispute is deleted or a statement is filed, it is your responsibility to request that anyone who has recently received your report be notified of the changes. Any inaccurate information that has been corrected or deleted on your credit report will be made within 30 days after the investigation is complete.

## Length Of Reporting Time

A credit reporting agency can not report negative information that is more than seven years old. Bankruptcies can be reported for up to ten years.

## Limited Access To Files

A credit reporting agency can only report information about you to people or organizations recognized by the FCRA. The most common people or organizations that have access to your information are creditors, insurers, employers, and landlords. In addition, anyone you give written approval to can access your credit report.

## 2. REQUESTING A FREE CREDIT REPORT

Credit reports are available at no charge in some instances. For example, if you will be graduating and plan to look for a job within 60 days, you can request a copy of your credit report at no charge. A complete list of criteria you must meet in order to qualify for a free credit report is listed on the next page. If you do not meet these conditions, a fee of up to $8 will be assessed for each request.

- A person/organization has taken action against you because of information supplied by the credit-reporting agency, and you request the report within 60 days of receiving notice of the action.
- You are unemployed and plan to seek employment within 60 days.
- You are on welfare.
- Your report is inaccurate due to fraud.

## 3. LOCATING A CREDIT REPORTING AGENCY

There are numerous credit reporting agencies available. Many provide their users specific information; however, some do provide an overall credit report. To locate one or more credit reporting agencies that meet your specific requirements, use a search engine on the Internet, contact a local bank or financial institution, or contact the state or federal consumer protection agency.

# PREPARING FOR YOUR CAREER

## CHAPTERS

# CAREER PREPARATION

The primary reason most people attend college is to prepare themselves for a career. Although a college degree is an important asset to have when you begin your career search, many employers are looking for much more from their candidates, particularly when there is a tight job market. That is why it is important to also develop various skills while attending college. This section will describe some of the most important skills employers are looking for and how you can obtain and/or develop them while attending college.

## 1. SKILLS THAT EMPLOYERS ARE LOOKING FOR
The more skills and talents you have to offer an employer, the more valuable and sought after you become. This section provides some of the most important skills and talents employers look for when they interview candidates. If your degree does not offer required courses that assist you in developing these skills or talents, consider taking elective courses that will.

**Work Experience**
Having relevant work experience is one of the first things an employer will check when reviewing a candidate's resume. Review the "Educational Employment" section on page 136 to learn more about programs designed to assist college students obtain relevant work experience.

**Communication**
Effective communication is essential in all aspects of your life, especially your career. Being able to effectively express your opinions and thoughts through your writing and speech will often outweigh weaknesses in other areas. Therefore, even if you believe you are a strong communicator, it is in

your best interest to take courses that develop these skills, such as public speaking, debate and business-writing courses.

## Teamwork
One of the more recent additions to effective business management is the implementation of teams. Companies want employees from every level of management working together to develop new ideas on how to save money, make new or better products, and solve internal problems. Because of the demand for teamwork skills from employers, colleges have begun to offer students the opportunity to develop these skills, such as group projects/assignments and intramural activities.

## Leadership
Leadership is probably the most difficult skill to teach because of the broad range of skills it encompasses. This difficulty has caused many employers to seek out candidates who have already acquired leadership skills. Although there are some colleges that offer courses in leadership, hands-on experience is often the best method of learning the skills of leadership. You can obtain this hands-on experience by accepting leadership positions within different organizations at your college, such as a club or intramural activity.

## Computer Knowledge
Understanding how to operate a computer is no longer what employers want from their candidates. To an employer, knowing how to operate a computer is just expected. Instead, employers want candidates who are familiar with the current software programs that are used within their industry. To help prepare students for this demand, most college programs offer their students access to the latest industry software packages. However, it is probably a good idea to contact industry trade associations and review industry publications to determine which software programs are currently being used in the industry. Since industry software programs can be extremely expensive, it may not be worth your personal investment. However, software companies will offer colleges access to their software at hugely discounted prices or even for free. If your college does not offer the latest industry software, contact the head of your department and request that the school offer access to it.

### Grade Point Average (GPA)

To an employer, having a high GPA is not only a sign of intelligence, but also a sign of a highly skilled student. Sure, there are some students who can easily obtain high grades without much effort, but for most students, in order to obtain a high GPA they must be a good time manager and an effective communicator, have strong self motivation, as well as a whole host of other valuable skills. If your GPA is below average or not as high as you would like it to be, contact your academic advisor and ask about courses that you can take to help learn the skills needed to become a better student.

### Motivation, Desire & Self-Discipline

Colleges rarely offer courses in motivation, desire or self-discipline. However, these are all skills that employers are looking for from their candidates. So where do you learn them, or better yet, how do you show an employer that you have them? These skills are learned over time and are demonstrated in your actions. For example, maintaining a high GPA, holding leadership positions in campus activities and working while attending college are all signs to an employer of a student who is motivated, has the desire to accomplish goals, and is self-disciplined.

## 2. NON-COLLEGIATE CAREER PREPARATION

In some cases, colleges may not offer courses you believe to be essential to your career. For example, if your career goal is to enter the field of software sales, employers in that field may consider you a particularly attractive candidate if you had already received training in professional sales and negotiation. Specialized training, such as professional sales and negotiation, can be obtained through a number of resources. Often industry trade associations and publications have information about organizations that offer this training. However, before investing in this type of training, contact potential employers in your industry and ask for their opinion about obtaining this training. In some cases, employers may want their employees to be trained in-house to avoid learning conflicting skills.

# EDUCATIONAL EMPLOYMENT

Educational employment programs, such as an internship, are an excellent way to learn about career opportunities that are available to you, make valuable contacts within an industry, develop your resume, and potentially provide you with a job opportunity after you graduate. Because of the value educational employment programs offer, you should participate in as many of them as possible. However, be aware that educational employment positions are highly competitive and can be difficult to obtain. This section will describe the different educational employment programs that are available, as well as provide you with tips on how to locate and make the most of them.

## 1. INTERNSHIPS

An internship is a short-term work experience in which students receive hands-on-training and experience in a career field. Internships can vary in length, but commonly coincide with college terms, such as a quarter or semester.

### Types Of Internships

- **Academic internships** are "for-credit" internships that are required by the college to be completed by students in order for the students to earn their degree. In other words, the internship is a required course that the student must pay for in order to graduate. In most cases, students rarely are compensated monetarily for participating in these types of internships. In addition, because the student is completing the internship for credit, they may be required to complete an assignment at the end of the internship in order to earn credit, such as writing a paper or performing a presentation about their experience.

- **Non-academic internships** are internships that are coordinated between the company and the student and do not involve any academic benefits, such as credits toward graduation. Monetary compensation is not guaranteed and is usually provided at the discretion of the company. Often, the more competitive an internship is, the more likely monetary compensation will not be offered.

## 2. COOPERATIVE EDUCATIONS (CO-OP)

Cooperative education programs are very similar to internships in what they have to offer for educational experience. However, unlike an internship, cooperative education programs usually last in length for more than one quarter or semester. Also, businesses that participate in cooperative education programs usually compensate the program participants monetarily.

### Types Of Cooperative Education
- **Alternating** cooperative education programs exist when the student works full-time for the participating business for a quarter or semester, and then the alternate quarter or semester, the student returns to school full-time.
- **Parallel** cooperate education programs exist when the student works for the participating business as well as attends school during the same term.

## 3. EXTERNSHIPS

An externship is a program developed so that a student can experience a quick view into the opportunities that exist within a major, business or industry. In most cases, an externship is developed so that the student can experience a "day-in-the-life" of a career they are interested in pursuing. The student is invited to follow the person around through the day, take notes, ask questions, and occasionally assist with small projects. Externships can be completed in as short time period as an afternoon or can last as long as a week or two. Most students complete externships during vacation periods from school, such as over Winter or Spring break.

Students are rarely provided any monetary or educational credit compensation for participating in an externship.

## 4. VOLUNTEERING

Volunteering your time and skills is a great way to help a needy organization as well as receive valuable experience. There are many ways to volunteer and many more organizations to choose from. If there is a particular organization you are interested in working with, contact them and ask about volunteer opportunities that exist. Because scheduling among volunteer organizations varies greatly, be sure to understand and ask what requirements you are required to perform as a volunteer.

## 5. SUMMER & PART-TIME JOBS

Although educational employment programs are a great way to get hands-on-experience, they are not your only options. Summer and part-time jobs can also be valuable tools for gaining educational experience. Before taking an ordinary part-time or summer job, do some research and determine what opportunities exist for jobs within your major or industry of interest. You may find that positions that interest you will most likely not be listed in the newspaper, bulletin boards or other standard job listing areas. Therefore, you will need to use your networking skills to locate these positions. See the "Networking" section on page 141 for more information.

## 6. LOCATING A POSITION

In most cases, companies that offer an educational employment position will only accept students that have completed at least two years of college. However, if you are interested in finding a position after completing your first year of college, do not be discouraged as there are a number of companies that will accept students with only one year of college experience. When you are ready to start locating an educational employment position, be sure to consider some of these tips.

- Prepare your resume and a standard cover letter. You may find it helpful to visit with your college's Career Resource Center for assistance in developing your resume and cover letter.
- Although your college's Career Resource Center is a great place to start searching for educational employment opportunities, do not rely on them as your only resource. Use your networking skills to locate other opportunities that may exist. See the "Networking" section on page 141.

- If there is a particular company that you would like to work for, visit with that company's Human Resource (HR) office directly to determine how to obtain an educational employment position. You may also find it helpful to visit directly with specific contacts within the company about opportunities that exist if the HR staff is not helpful.

## 7. SELECTING A POSITION

When you have the chance to accept an educational employment position, be sure to consider what you will gain from the experience before accepting. If the position does not offer the experiences you were hoping for, consider locating another position. Below are some tips to consider as you evaluate educational employment opportunities.

- Request a detailed job description and read it thoroughly. If you have questions about any part of it, be sure to ask for clarification before accepting the position.
- Determine whom you will be working with as well as their positions within the organization.
- Ask about the type of projects you will be working on as well as the projects that have been completed by previous students.
- Ask what compensation, if any, you will be provided and how often monetary disbursements will be made. Avoid accepting a position based on monetary compensation alone. There are many other forms of compensation to consider, such as educational credit and relevant work experience.
- Visit with current or past students who have already worked in the position you are considering accepting.

## 8. MAKING THE MOST OF YOUR NEW POSITION

After you accept a new position, particularly an educational employment opportunity, you should make the most of that position. Listed below are just a few ways to accomplish this task.

- Treat your new position as if it was your career.
- As with any position, dress appropriately, address other co-workers with respect, and avoid conflicts.
- Request assistance if you are confused about an assignment or task. Remember, you are new and are not expected to know everything.
- Demonstrate your skills and talents in every project you are assigned.
- Ask for constructive criticism on completed projects.

- Collect references prior to completing your position and maintain contact with them. You never know when you may need their assistance or when they may have information to share with you.
- Network with as many people as possible. Refer to the "Networking" section on page 141.
- When you complete an assignment, request an additional assignment as soon as possible to show your interest and enthusiasm.

# NETWORKING

Networking is a term commonly used to refer to the act of creating personal and professional relationships for the purpose of exchanging information, advice, contacts, or support.  Although the tips in this section will help you in acquiring various types of information through networking, this section will primarily focus on using networking for the purposes of collecting information about different career choices and finding that perfect job.

## 1.  WHY IS NETWORKING IMPORTANT?
Think of networking as compiling a large amount of personal assistants that are available for your use to help you complete your task.  The more personal assistants you have, the more information you gather and the easier your task becomes.  When it comes to finding a job, the more people you have looking for job opportunities for you, the more choices you have to consider.

## 2.  NETWORKING RESOURCES
The amount of networking resources available to you is almost endless.  Never underestimate the value of your resources.  You never know who may hold the key to the information you need.  Below are just a few examples of networking resources available to you.

### Classmates, Friends, Relatives & Neighbors
Your personal networking resources are often your best resources.  Not only are they easier to utilize, but often they also have a personal interest in seeing that you accomplish your goals.  When collecting information about different career choices or locating a job, let these people know what

information you are in need of and ask them if they can offer you any assistance. Providing them a copy of your resume is also a good idea, because you never know whom they may come in contact with.

## Recent Graduates

Recent graduates, particularly those in your area of study, are also a great resource for networking. These people have already done a lot of the work that you are trying to accomplish and can provide you valuable information on who to contact or where to look for information. Contact your academic advisor, professors or your college's Career Service and Alumni offices to assist you in locating recent graduates.

## Academic Advisors & Professors

Academic advisors and professors in your area of study have a wealth of contacts that can be of assistance to you in your career search. These people are often in contact with professionals in their field of study and can direct you to some of the best resources available.

## Career Resource Center

Because the Career Resource Center is the primary location where employers start their search for new employees, it is in your best interest to make plenty of contacts at this location. The more interaction you have with the staff at the Career Resource Center, the better chance you have that your name will come up when the staff is asked if they know of any qualified candidates for a position. If at all possible, try to get to know the Director of the Career Resource Center. You can do this by scheduling an appointment with this person to discuss your career goals. Since this person is often the primary contact for employers at your school, they may have access to valuable information that may not necessarily be available to all students.

## Alumni Association

Not only does your Alumni Association often have access to contact information of alumni in the career field that you are looking for, but they also have access to businesses that support the association financially. Because of their resources and contacts, it would be in your best interest to try to schedule a meeting with the Director of the Alumni Association. Let this person know what your goals are and ask them for their advice. Also be sure to ask them if you can provide them a copy of your resume. You never know whom they may come in contact with.

## Professional Associations & Conferences
Professional associations exist for almost every career field. These groups are a great resource for information and contacts because they produce informational publications, membership directories, and job listings. In addition, many professional associations host conferences for their members as an opportunity to provide the members access to the latest industry information. Discounted rates are usually available for students.

## The Internet
The Internet can be a valuable tool for networking and gathering information. On-line discussion groups, chat rooms and web-based networks are all great resources. To help find Internet resources that are best for you, visit with some of the groups mentioned above for their recommendations, as well as conduct your own search.

## Career/Job Fairs
Career/job fairs are a great place to make contacts and learn about opportunities in your field of study. Most colleges host their own career/job fairs, as do metropolitan areas. If you are interested in working in a region other than where your college is located, it may be worth your time to participate in career/job fairs in the region where you intend to live after college. To learn more about career/job fairs in other regions, contact colleges and local Chamber of Commerce offices in that region. In addition, have your school's Career Resource Center inquire of other schools' career fairs. When you do attend a career/job fair, avoid limiting your contacts to the obvious businesses in your field of study. There are often numerous businesses from every sector of the business world in attendance at these events. Take advantage of this opportunity and visit with businesses you do not know much about to learn about the opportunities that they have to offer.

## 3. HOW TO NETWORK
Networking, like any skill, takes time to develop. The more opportunities you have to network, the better you will become. Listed on the next page are a few points to consider in helping you network successfully.

**Obtaining A Networking Appointment**

- Before contacting people to network with, create a twenty to thirty-second introduction about yourself and why you want to meet with them. Avoid stating you are looking for a job. Instead, tell the person that you are there to gather information about their position, business and the industry.
- Be prepared to provide responses if they hesitate to schedule a meeting with you. For example, if they state that they cannot meet with you because they are too busy, do not give up. In many cases, people use that response as a way to determine your level of interest. Therefore, instead of quitting, try pursuing their response with a little flattery. For instance, inform them that you understand that they are busy and if they were not, you probably would not be calling them to visit with them.
- If you were referred to a contact by a personal acquaintance, mention that person's name in your conversation when arranging an appointment. This may be the key to getting the meeting.
- Stress that your schedule is flexible, and that you are willing to meet at a time that is convenient for their schedule.
- If the contact is just not willing to schedule a one-on-one meeting, suggest visiting with them on the telephone or sending the person a few questions via email.
- If the contact is difficult to reach on the telephone, consider writing a letter requesting a meeting and then follow-up with a telephone message requesting a meeting time. Be sure to provide your contact information in your letter to assist the person in contacting you.
- After scheduling an appointment, be sure to thank the contact for the opportunity to visit, and reconfirm the date, time and meeting location. Also be sure to provide the person a telephone number to reach you in case they need to reschedule.

**Preparing For A Networking Appointment**

- Research information about the contact, their company and the industry they work in. The more information you know about the person, the more impressed they will be with you, and the more information they will be willing to share with you.

- Dress and act appropriately. For example, if you are meeting at the person's place of business, dress in business attire.
- Develop two or three introductory questions that will assist you in starting a conversation, such as questions about the person's business, background or a common interest.
- Have specific questions written down that you would like answered and have materials with you to take notes. The following are a few sample questions you may want to ask.
  1.   Describe a typical day at work.
  2.   How many hours do you normally work in a week?
  3.   What do you see as the potential for growth in this field?
  4.   What can I do in order to obtain employment in this field?
  5.   Would you advise people to enter this career area? Why or why not?
  6.   Knowing what you know at this point in your career, would you take the same job again? Why or why not?

## Conducting A Networking Appointment
- During the introductions, request the contact's business card and offer your's in return. Your college's Career Resource Center may offer students the ability to order college business cards. If not, consider purchasing your own from an office supply store or make them yourself with a business card software program.
- Remember the contact's name and use it frequently during the conversation.
- Be enthusiastic and show interest in the information that the person is providing.
- If the person you are visiting with offers you additional contact names, be sure to ask them for their permission to use their name as a reference when contacting those contacts.
- Thank the person for their time and, if appropriate, ask them if you can share your resume with them.

## After Completing A Networking Appointment
- Send the person a thank-you letter within 24 to 48 hours.
- If appropriate, maintain contact with the person and provide them an occasional update on your progress. Also, if the contact provided you

additional contact names, be sure to inform them of your progress in visiting with those contacts.

**Attending A Networking Function**
Career/Job fairs and industry meetings are just a few examples of great locations for networking. Networking at these types of functions is very similar to a networking appointment, except for the fact that your time with a contact will be a lot shorter and less organized. When attending a networking function, you may find some of these tips helpful.
- Research the event and determine who will be attending. Gather as much information as possible about the key contacts you would like to meet.
- Use contacts you already know at the event to introduce you to new contacts. If you do not know anyone at the event, introduce yourself to people and inform them of why you are there. Although this may seem scary, you will be surprised at how people will be willing to help you out.
- When you meet new contacts, request a business card from them and offer them your business card in return. After completing your conversation with them, take relevant notes on the back of their business cards to assist you in recalling important information about them.
- Bring several copies of your resume with you. If appropriate, ask the contacts that you meet if you can provide them a copy.
- After attending the networking function, review the information you gathered and make detailed notes on the contacts that you met with.
- If there are contacts that you had met at the function that you would like to visit with again, write them a short letter thanking them for their time at the function. Also, be sure to state that you would like to visit with them again to gather additional information and will be contacting them soon to schedule a meeting.

## 4. NETWORKING AFTER GRADUATION
As you will find out, networking is an extremely valuable skill to use in locating a job after graduation. However, networking does not stop at that point. In fact, networking is a skill that should be utilized throughout your life. Continue to make new contacts and assist others as they network. You never know who may be able to assist you in the future.

# From the Authors of Life During College:

**ISBN:** 097009440X
**Suggested Retail Price:** $10.95
(Discounts Available for Quantity Purchases)

For Additional Information Visit:

**www.LifeAfterGraduation.com**